FROM

ATTIC TO CELLAR

OR

HOUSEKEEPING MADE EASY.

BY

MRS. ELIZABETH F. HOLT.

SALEM:
THE SALEM PRESS PUBLISHING AND PRINTING CO.
The Salem Press.
1892.

CONTENTS.

PREFACE.

A PRACTICAL knowledge of the details of housekeeping is as necessary to insure success in making a home, as for any business in which one engages, and the woman who finds herself at the head of a household without this knowledge is in need of all the assistance that the experience of others can give her.

It is not the purpose of this work to give anything in the line of cooking. There are many valuable cook books already in the market, which have been issued for that purpose.

The book is designed to give practical help in the daily routine of household work to women who are in need of such knowledge. Several of these papers have been published in the *Household*.

CHAPTER I.

THE KITCHEN.

THE kitchen is the centre of the household and from it will radiate comfort or discomfort for every member of the family. It should be the first room to receive attention when furnishing a house. Unfortunately, it is often the last.

Young people about to marry usually commence with the parlor and end with the kitchen, using whatever money is left for that room. This is a mistake which they soon discover themselves. The kitchen ought to be planned for first.

If onc has but a limited amount for furnishing a house it would be well to portion it out for each room, according to the importance that these rooms will exercise over the comfort of the inmates, and then take the amount decided upon, and go over the rooms separately, making a list of things actually necessary, leaving the ornamental entirely out of consideration. It is astonishing to note how even bare necessities will count up.

With most of the modern houses that are rented the range is usually included; when this is not the case, a good range will take quite a little of the amount devoted to the kitchen.

Do not forget any of the labor-saving machines; rather retrench if need be in the furnishings of the parlor, or the china for the table, than in the kitchen, especially if for economy one is not able to command good service and the mistress must do a part of the work for the household.

The kitchen is the foundation of the health and happiness of the family, and every housekeeper should have it under strict surveillance, and insist that it is kept neat and clean.

As the large majority of women cannot have a kitchen built for them, but must make the best of the one they already have, it is useless to go into the details of an ideal kitchen.

But a small proportion of women are favored with a large sunny room that can be easily ventilated. They must therefore use judgment and common sense to invent ways and means of counteracting any deficiency that may exist in their particular kitchen.

Perhaps the most important requisite is good ventilation. The air should be changed frequently if the room is small, as it soon becomes vitiated with the smoke, stove gas, odor from cooking, and drainage from the sink, combined with the exhalations from the lungs of the occupants.

Every kitchen ought to contain two tables: one for use as a dining table for the servant, and another larger one for cooking purposes, which need not be the regulation kitchen table with drop leaf and one or two drawers, but should be made of pine, by a carpenter according to measurement of the space that can be spared for it, and the top of it should be covered with white enamelled cloth, that is easily kept clean.

The lower part, instead of being provided with

legs, can be utilized for shelves, drawers and cupboards for holding kitchen utensils.

In the drawers may be kept tin measuring cups, potato masher, lemon squeezer, egg beaters, kitchen knives, forks and spoons, can-opener, corkscrew, mixing spoons, etc.

On the shelves there should be room for a bowl of sifted pastry flour, and another one of bread flour. Salt, spices, baking powder, sugar and other ingredients, should also find a place there.

The cupboards will accommodate the buckets of graham, rye and Indian meal, and hooks about the side will be convenient for hanging gem and biscuit pans.

There should be some thought given to the construction of such a table, that it may be planned with reference to each one's special and individual need.

A chest of drawers in a kitchen will be found a great convenience for holding kitchen table linen, towels, dish cloths, strainers, etc., and an adjustable shelf attached to the wall by means of hinges, with a piece of wood below it, that can turn out forming a support, will make an excellent ironing table, which can be let down against the wall when not required for use.

Directly over this can be placed two shelves made with partitions for holding flat irons, stands, holders, cloths for wiping irons, wax, clothes sprinkler, etc. A linen curtain suspended from a brass rod attached to the shelves, will keep the contents free from dust, and it can be easily laundered when necessary.

In many homes, housework is mere drudgery simply because no thought has been given to the arrangement and furnishings. A woman's workshop ought to be as well supplied with working tools as her husband's is.

If the floor of the kitchen is of soft wood an oil cloth is almost a necessity unless it is painted, but nearly all modern kitchens are provided with a hard wood floor which can be easily washed and kept clean.

In front of the range there should be a piece

of zinc fully a yard square. This can be scoured frequently and is a safeguard against pieces of hot coal which often drop from the stove.

Near the range, a set of towel supports that can be lowered or raised as needed, should be firmly screwed to the wall, for the accommodation of wet dish cloths, towels, etc.

Brooms, brushes and dust-pans should not be hung on the inside of the closet door where they will rattle or fall whenever it is opened or shut.

If there is no small closet near the kitchen that can be devoted to them, let the carpenter make one sufficiently large to contain these, also the ironing board, clothes basket and clothes-pin bag.

Brooms ought never to stand in a corner as they soon get bent and out of shape. A stout cord for hanging them by should be placed in the handle.

An oil stove will be found a great convenience as well as an economy at certain times. During the hot summer weather it is desirable to dispense with the fire in the range, and an oil stove that is well constructed, if used with care and kept clean, will last many years.

Keep the ice chest as near the kitchen as possible ; it will save many steps.

If there is a closet under your sink, as there is in most houses that have not been built recently, remove it, and find a place elsewhere for the pots, kettles, dish cloth and stove blacking utensils that are usually kept there. In too many kitchens it is a receptacle for damp rags and a breeding place for water bugs and cockroaches.

If there are no up-stairs windows in a neighbor's house in close proximity for overlooking your kitchen, it will be found better to dispense with shades and supply the lower half of the window with cross-barred muslin sash curtains that can be easily laundered ; the upper part of the window to be left uncovered for light, air, and better ventilation.

Three strong wooden chairs, and one comfortable wooden rocking chair should be included in the kitchen furniture.

In regard to the articles needed for culinary purposes, one's purse and the size of the family must regulate their number. Whatever can be purchased in granite ware rather than tin or iron ware will prove in the end economy of time as well as money, for granite ware is easily kept clean, and does not need to be scoured.

It is not well to have too many large dishes; they are not easily handled and the smaller saucepans and bowls are more convenient.

Anything that will save labor should be planned for. As a general thing a cook or general housemaid will appreciate "the conveniences" as much as you do yourself, and it may help to make the vexed question of domestic service an easier problem for you.

CHAPTER II

BED ROOMS.

THE craze for littering a house with ornaments and bric-a-brac, of crowding every available square inch of floor room with furniture, that an artistic and home-like appearance may be obtained, has been carried to excess.

Simplicity and utility can be combined with beauty in a way that will express individuality and refinement in the home, without the meaningless array of tidies and sofa pillows too fine to rest one's head against, befrilled lamp shades, that exclude the light, and foot cushions that are stumbling blocks to those whose eyesight is defective.

If there is any calling in which there is a wide field for women, it is architecture. In the average home, the chambers are often the smallest and most inconvenient rooms in the house, situated perhaps on the shady side, with no definite place planned for the bed, which must frequently be where the wind will blow directly on the sleeper's head if the one window is left open at night.

When we take into consideration the fact that about one-third of our lives is spent in our sleeping rooms, it would seem imperative that we give earnest thought and attention to the requirements necessary for the health of the occupants.

Rooms situated on the north side of the house, should never be used as chambers except for guests who occupy them only occasionally. The lack of sunshine and good ventilation in a chamber is sufficient of itself to account for many of the ills with which we are afflicted.

For suburban residences it will be found that a small veranda protected from the gaze of passers, and that opens from a chamber window, will be of great advantage in airing and purifying the bed-clothing.

At least once a week pillow-slips should be removed, the pillows beaten with a rattan beater, and left for an hour in the air, where the sun will not shine directly upon them, as the heat of the sun will draw out the oil from the feathers. If there is no veranda, the clothes line in the yard, although not so convenient, will answer the purpose.

The bed ought to be so arranged that one can go around it without moving it from place in order to make it up.

Physicians assert that it is not healthful to sleep near the wall on account of dampness, and also because one's breath is thrown back from a wall, and inhaled again.

Children should not sleep with adults and especially not with an elderly person.

It is considered far more healthful for grown people to occupy different beds. The air which surrounds the body under the bed clothing is exceedingly impure, being impregnated with the poisonous substances which have escaped through the pores of the skin. Celebrated physicians have condemned the double bed.

It is said that no two persons can sleep in this way regularly for any length of time, without feeling ill effects from it. The more robust person is sure to draw nervous force from the more delicate one.

Two small bedsteads will not take much more space than a double bed. It is seldom that two people require the same amount of clothing over them, and with two beds this can be more easily regulated.

If there is any one thing in house furnishing where a housewife is justified in being extravagant it is in the appointments for the bed. Easy springs, a good hair mattress, and soft warm blankets, are conducive to healthful sleep, and a good promoter of happiness.

Strong, plain, substantial-looking furniture which is easily kept clean, will prove more satisfactory in the long run, than either the carved, or the graceful slender styles which look more attractive in the salesrooms.

If brass bedsteads are too expensive, an iron bedstead painted white, with draperies of white dotted muslin and an all white dressing, is not only pretty and dainty to look upon, but is commended to housekeepers because it is easy to keep in order — the furnishings can be readily laundered and a fresh coat of paint will make it look like new.

Now that the set bowls in bedrooms have been so generally condemned as unhealthful, more attention has been paid to the construction of the wash stand. The large ones are much more convenient than those of smaller size.

There should be ample room for the pitcher to stand beside the bowl, so that it need not be lifted from it when water is needed and it is desirable to have plenty of space for glycerine, bay rum and tooth powder bottles, as well as the other belongings of the toilet set.

In a bed room above all other rooms do not carpet the floor. A hard wood floor provided with a few rugs is best, both on account of neatness and health. The carpet conceals an enormous amount of refuse, and tells no tales of what it harbors.

Where there is no hard wood floor the cracks may be first filled with putty, and the floor stained and finished with an oil finish, or it may be painted.

There should be no portieres in a bed room and the draperies should be of thin cotton texture that can be often laundered. The less furniture in the room, the better. Rattan or willow chairs with removable cushions that are covered with some cotton material are desirable.

A screen high enough to protect one from the draught of an open window at night is almost as necessary as a bedstead.

Those who are fortunate enough to be able to build their house as they choose, if they follow the advice of eminent physicians, will not paper the walls of their bed rooms, which should be finished in hard plaster with a smooth finish and then tinted—nor will they paint the woodwork, which should be of hard wood, and finished in oil.

The rooms set apart foı the use of the servant, are generally speaking, small, cold and cheerless. Often there is only a skylight for admitting air and light.

When there is one window the bed may be of necessity so near it that it cannot be opened at night for proper ventilation, and in consequence the occupant must breathe poisoned air through the hours when she should be getting rest and strength for the coming day's work.

Is it to be wondered at that she is often ill-natured and irritable during the day, or that she is inclined to slight her work if her head aches, and get through with it as easily as she can? Many mistresses have been known to do the same.

When it is necessary through lack of good sleeping rooms, that a servant should occupy such a one as referred to, a tall screen should be provided that will effectually protect the head of the sleeper from the air.

The servant's rooms should be furnished mainly with reference to sanitary conditions. If possible the walls should be painted instead of papered a warm light tint that will brighten the room and make it seem home-like.

The floor should be painted with the brownish yellow shade which is cheerful looking and wears well.

Onc breadth of carpeting should be tacked across the room beside the bed, and a small rug or mat placed before the wash stand and bureau.

A closet is a necessity and if the room is not provided with it, a temporary one should be manufactured by means of a shelf and curtain.

The bed should be a single one of iron and of the simplest construction, that it may be easily cleaned. It should be provided with a woven wire spring and a mattress. One made entirely of cotton is very comfortable, or an excelsior mattress with cotton top and bottom will answer the purpose and is inexpensive.

One feather pillow of moderate size is sufficient for a single bed.

The sheets and pillow slips may be of unbleached cotton if preferred for wear. Blankets instead of comfortables should be provided for bedding as it is necessary that they be washed often. Also a white honeycomb spread which is inexpensive, and so light that it is as easily laundered as a sheet.

A high-back rocking chair with arms, such as are commonly used for piazza will be found very comfortable for a girl to rest in when she is tired and goes to her room. This, with one common cane-seated chair is sufficient if only one servant occupies the room; if there are two, another single bed should be provided, also an extra rocking chair, plain chair, bureau and wash stand.

When it is possible to give servants separate rooms it should be done, as there will be greater harmony between them, and less "talking over" their mistress; but where this is an impossibility separate beds ought in all cases to be provided.

Cheese-cloth curtains finished with a broad hem and looped back with bands of the same are very inexpensive, can be easily laundered and will add much to the attractive appearance of the room.

A white linen cover plainly hemmed, with a good-sized pin cushion filled with pins resting on it is suggestive of a homelike feeling. And a set of cheap pine book shelves screwed to the wall, which will hold an alarm clock, a few books and perhaps a few prized possessions that are ordinarily kept in the owner's trunk, may go a great way toward making a girl feel contented with the quarters into which she has drifted, and perhaps stimulate her to do her best to retain her place, and merit the good will of her employer.

CHAPTER III.

OTHER ROOMS IN THE HOUSE.

YOU can often judge more accurately of a family by their dining room than by their parlor. It is not always the finest table-linen or the choicest china that betokens refinement, or that gives an inviting "homey" look to the table. The personality of the mistress is plainly stamped here, and the purse has very little to do with it.

It will be economy to purchase a strong substantial dining room table and chairs that will last many years. Omit the sideboard if necessary rather than purchase one at the expense of the more necessary furnishings.

The same may be said of all the furniture that you purchase. Select it with a view to keeping it, not to disposing of it when you feel you can afford anything better. Rather purchase the different articles piece by piece and bide your time, even if your home does have a bare unfurnished look about it.

The most hospitable woman of my acquaintance lives in a small old-fashioned house that has a little box of a dining room, without even a sideboard to grace it, and yet I have never seen one in any grand establishment which has home happiness and refinement so plainly written upon it.

Every Saturday night it is well understood by her friends that they are at liberty to drop in to supper, and there are many to avail themselves of this privilege although the bill of fare for this night never varies from one year's end to the other.

They always know that there will be beans and brown bread cooked in the good old fashioned way, delicious coffee with cream, and light feathery biscuits with melted maple sugar.

Not an elaborate menu certainly or an expensive one, but one is sure to meet delightful people there, and the hostess is the most popular little woman of my acquaintance.

I was there one Saturday evening when there were nine friends who had "dropped in" and I became a little uneasy for our hostess, who sat chatting as unconcernedly as if she had the resources of a hotel to draw upon.

I need not have had any fears, as I afterwards learned, for sufficient beans and brown bread were always provided for fifteen people baked the previous day in order that "reception night," as it was called in the family, might not be too much of a tax on the one housemaid.

They were warmed over before supper, and what was left did duty for Monday morning's breakfast, and for soup Tuesday at dinner.

The children of the hostess, a little girl and boy, ten and twelve years old, always waited on the table "reception night" and better service I have seldom seen.

"We believe it is an education for them," their mother said one day when referring to it; "for it has taught them to be quick in their movements, and attentive to the wants of the guests, and with it all they are interested in the conversation and enjoy it.

I could not expect the maid to cook and wait upon our guests at the same time, so we have tried to make a virtue of necessity and the children are delighted to do it, and enjoy our Saturday nights as much as we do."

This wise mother is a thorough housekeeper, and understands the value of system in the work of the household—that the kitchen is responsible for success in the dining room, that it is good for us to gather friends about our table, and that in order to be able to do this we must know the possibilities of every dollar in the way of food, and what it is right for us to spend in that way.

The result is that, with a small income they have a home around which is an atmosphere of love, happiness, comfort and hospitality, which one insensibly feels when they enter the house.

A sewing room is by no means the necessity in

a house that a dining room is, but if there is a small room that can be set apart for this purpose, much practical use and comfort may be obtained from it, which would readily be appreciated by those who are not so situated that they can indulge in this luxury, and must make use of bed room or sitting room for the family sewing.

It is the one room in the house which should be thoroughly practical. It should have no carpet, no draperies, no extra furniture, and nothing in the way of bric-a-brac or ornaments of any kind, unless they are made to serve a purpose.

It needs a chest of drawers, a dining room table, a small cutting table that can be folded up, a paper lap-board, a sewing machine, a dress form, one or two sewing chairs and a footstool.

Besides these almost necessary articles of furniture there are bags or pockets, made of stout denim or cretonne, for patterns, pieces of cloth, woolen pieces, braids, tapes, etc., which are made like shoe-bags, to be hung on the inside of the closet door.

A scrap-basket and a rag bag are both necessary. The latter can be made of cretonne or denim, so that it can be hung in the room in plain sight instead of the closet where it usually crowds other clothing and is troublesome to get at.

A sewing room ought to be a place where one can cut and litter to any degree that seems necessary, and feel that it will be no great task to make the room tidy again.

There are as many varieties of "guest chambers" as there are housekeepers, and it does not always follow that the one which affords most comfort to the tired traveller is found in the home where wealth is abundant.

The bed is the most important article of furniture, and should receive the most careful oversight and attention from the hostess.

If the income is limited, purchase a cheap, painted set of furniture, and put the larger share of the money that you have appropriated for the furnishings of this room into a good set of springs, mattress and pillows for the bed.

Be sure that the sheets are long enough to tuck in firmly at the foot, the blankets wide enough to cover the bed and reach a little distance over the sides, that there are a sufficient number of them, with an extra cover for the one whose circulation is poor, and never mind about the sham bolster tied up with bows at the end, or the ruffled pillow-slips, or the embroidered spread, if to purchase them you must scrimp on some of the essentials of the bed. The bed should always be freshly made when occupied, as it draws dampness if not aired every day, and this is one reason why many people take cold when going away from home to sleep.

If all the appointments of the wash-stand be complete and satisfactory, your guest will not feel disturbed if the china is of the plainest and cheapest white ware.

If the room is lighted by electricity be sure that the method is thoroughly understood by the guest. If there is any peculiarity in regard to the burner of the lamp, explain it, and place a candle with matches on a stand by the bed, so that light may be had without rising if necessary.

Have a clock in the room that will keep good time, and see to it yourself that it is wound, informing your guest the hour for breakfast, and also ascertaining if he wishes to be called in the morning.

With such a guest-chamber one need have no fear for the comfort of "the stranger within our gates," even if there are no pretty draperies or costly rugs, or any of the dainty appointments that wealth can purchase, and which are by no means to be despised or omitted if the income will warrant it.

Rugs, pictures, books and ornaments add much to the attractive appearance of the room.

An easy rocking chair, hassock or stool, a little bookcase and a good lamp go far towards giving the room a cosey and homelike air.

If to these can be added, a writing desk or table fully equipped with writing material, a work basket fitted with thimble, needles, white cotton, sewing silk and linen thread, scissors, boot buttons, etc., it will approach nearer to the ideal guest chamber that almost every woman has at some time pictured for herself.

The thing to be avoided is a superfluity of ornaments which are only in the way and which the guest has a wholesome dread of breaking.

There should be nothing in a guest chamber that is too good to be used, but kind thoughts manifested in these small attentions to the comfort and welfare of a guest are as much of a welcome as words.

If there are children in your home, and there is a room that you can spare for them as a nursery, do so, for it will give happiness to them, and comfort to yourself. Let it be their room exclusively, and do not because it is a sunny room put plants in the windows, but leave them for the little ones to look out of whenever they choose.

Paint the floor a warm sunshiny tint and scatter a few mats or rugs about it.

Get a packing box for the little girls to make into a doll's house, and another for the boys to convert into a stable, freight-house, or whatever they prefer.

If the boys are old enough to know the use of carpenters' tools, put a wooden bench in one corner, and a box to hold a screw-driver, hammer, tacks, awl, saw and plane.

Screw some shelves on the wall, low enough for the children to reach the books on them. Let the boy's books be kept there, the story books for the girls, Mother Goose, and the picture and scrap books.

Have as little furniture as possible in the room, and have that little, strong and plain. A round table with castors, that may be pushed about easily, and on it a small basket, with needles, scissors and thread, for dollie's clothes.

There should be an extra pair of blunt pointed scissors, and a bottle of mucilage on the table for the pictures in magazines that are to be transferred to the scrap book, and a tray to hold numerous odds and ends of lead and slate pencils, bits of chalk, etc.

A blackboard, and one or two school room desks and seats, will add to the happiness of the children, who, almost universally, enjoy playing school.

Let them make all the noise they wish to there, and invite their little playfellows to join them.

The charm and freedom of this room will be a bright spot for the children to look back upon when they are "men and women grown tall."

In regard to the parlor, let it be the last room furnished, but exercise all the taste and judgment that you have, in the furnishing; bearing in mind that the sense of comfort in your belongings and the feeling that they are not too nice or too delicate for use, will far outweigh in the long run any feeling of pride in a dainty artistic-looking room which is charming as a reception room for your callers, but not practical as a living room for your family.

CHAPTER IV.

MISTRESS AND MAID.

ONE of the most difficult things that a housekeeper must meet is the servant question.

How often do we hear women say, "If I were strong enough to do the work of the household I would do it, and be independent."

But even with the requisite amount of strength and the most favorable conditions, unless circumstances render it necessary, it is not a desirable thing to give up a good part of one's life to the mere routine drudgery of housework.

It is seldom that one has the good fortune to secure a servant who has been trained under a competent and systematic housekeeper, and it is usually the case that one must begin with the foundation, if good service is required, even when a most satisfactory reference is forthcoming.

If the mistress exacts from herself a conscientious attention to detail, she is an example to those who serve her, and may with reason expect the same from them.

A servant respects a capable mistress and will work better for such a one, provided other things are equal.

The carelessness of the maid often reflects the carelessness of the mistress, and one who recognizes the fact that the tone of her household will depend largely upon her own idea of what it ought to be, possesses a wisdom that will stand her in good stead.

It is generally conceded among experienced housekeepers, that it is not wise to engage a middle-aged woman unless you have personal knowledge of such a one, for the reason that desirable servants of long experience are not apt to be looking for situations, but are passed from one friend's household to another.

When a servant is engaged her work should be fully stated and carefully explained, that she may understand exactly what is expected of her.

If the washings are large, if the family entertain beyond what is usual, if her work includes any care of the furnace, say so frankly. It is a purely business-like engagement, in which the maid should understand the service required for the wages offered.

Another important point to be settled in the beginning is what is commonly understood among servants as "privileges." These of course must be largely decided by the needs of the household, bearing in mind the fact that kitchen life is monotonous, and that church-going, and the afternoons and evenings out, are the only breaks in a week of servitude.

In regard to church-going, the work ought to be so arranged that each servant can have an opportunity to attend church every Sunday, and, nothing, except illness in the family, should be allowed to interfere with this arrangement.

When a general housework girl is the only servant, it is usual to allow her a week day afternoon and evening and a Sunday afternoon and evening in alternate weeks.

If it is possible to give these two afternoons and evenings every week, it will afford the maid greater pleasure, and make her better contented with her situation.

If, in addition to this, another evening in the week is granted, it is all that any maid ought to expect, or a mistress accord, except on special occasions.

Ten o'clock at night is late enough for any girl to be out of doors, and this hour for coming home should be rigidly insisted upon.

Until a servant has been proved and tried, a mistress ought to keep money and valuables under lock and key, with a strict watch over all her possessions.

In families where there is more than one domestic, the question of the division of work is often a hard one to solve. No general rule can be given, because the number of inmates, children and guests, are factors that enter into the consideration.

Where there are a cook and waitress, the cook is expected to take charge of the kitchen, and whatever pertains to it, to do the cooking, wash the common dishes, and assist with the washing and ironing.

The waitress attends to the upper portion of the house, waits at table, answers the bell, cleans silver, washes the glass, silver and china ware, assists with the washing and ironing, and usually takes care of the vestibule piazza and front door steps.

There are minor duties that are divided between the servants according to the judgment of the mistress, but a perfect understanding in regard to them should exist from the beginning.

When there are a cook and waitress to share the work between them the same privileges should be extended to each, and their time for going out so arranged that one of them shall always be in the house.

If an in-door man-servant is kept, he relieves

the maid of the vestibule piazza, etc., and attends to the fires, carves, and waits at table.

When there are young children, the duties of a nurse are so varied in different families, that they must be governed entirely by the requirements, and privileges accorded in like manner.

If the establishment is sufficiently large for keeping an in-door man-servant, a laundress is usually in the service also, unless the family laundry is attended to outside the house.

Where there is no laundress, it is customary for each maid to attend to her own personal washing and ironing.

A woman who shows due regard for her servants' welfare and comfort, and when appealed to takes an interest in their personal affairs without suggesting any unbecoming familiarity with them, will be able eventually to find servants who will appreciate such a home.

If a mistress sets her standard high she will find those in service who will come up to it, but the mistress who will put up with poor service, rather than take the trouble to make a change, is doing harm not only as regards the comfort of her household, but she is countenancing in her maid, something that should be reproved.

When we pay an incompetent servant the same wages that we would pay to one who gives us better service, we are putting a premium upon incompetency, and creating trouble for the next mistress.

A woman just as surely needs self-control, patience and tact to be a good mistress, as to be a good mother.

If fault must be found, it should not be shirked because of the unpleasantness attending it, but it should be done in a quiet, dignified way, and a proper time chosen for it. Let it be understood that you mean what you say, and obedience will follow, except in incorrigible cases.

The trouble is, that in our desire to get along as easily as we can, we are apt at times to shut our eyes to things that ought to call for reproof.

On the other hand, we may be too exacting.

When there is but one servant, and the house is large, it is well to remember that one pair of hands can not do everything, and a little kindly consideration, with judicious praise where it is deserved, will do something toward making the machinery move easily.

After all there is not such a tremendous difference between mistress and maid in the power to appreciate the comfort of a good home.

If we look about us, we shall find that the tried and faithful servant is the one who has a comfortable room, whose mistress is a good housekeeper, and who is paid fairly good wages.

CHAPTER V.

HOW TO TRAIN A WAITRESS.

BREAKFAST.

WHEREVER a waitress is employed, each meal should be served with care, and attention should be given to detail, otherwise a mistress would not feel at ease when guests are present at her table, neither could a maid perform satisfactorily what is required in table service without the experience and confidence that daily routine will give to her.

A waitress should have at least three light print dresses, two dark colored ones, six long white aprons, and a pair of low shoes, with light soles for house wear.

The caps are usually supplied by the mistress.

Three of these are sufficient and should be simply made that they may be easily laundered.

The maid should wear a light print dress in the morning, with a white cap, and long white apron—this apron to be changed when she waits upon the table for a fresher one kept for that purpose alone. This should be rigidly insisted upon, as one of the chief requisites of a waitress is that she look fresh and tidy, especially at the table.

The dress, cap and apron should be changed in the afternoon, two sets being kept for that Purpose, those used in the morning to be laundered each week, and those in the afternoon to be used in the morning of the next week.

This arrangement, with a dark print dress for washing days and gingham aprons to be slipped over the white apron for certain parts of the work, has been found generally satisfactory for ensuring a tidy appearance at all times.

A waitress should rise early enough to put the dining-room in order before the table is laid for breakfast. The windows should be opened the first thing, the room thoroughly aired, the floor brushed and the furniture dusted.

The table is then covered with a white cotton felt that comes for this purpose, and care should be used in placing the table cloth evenly over this, that it may not present a crooked appearance, or that one corner may not be lower than the other.

If fruit is to be served for the first course it should be placed in the centre of the table, and for each person should be placed a fruit plate upon which is a fruit doily, a finger bowl containing a little warm water, a silver fruit knife at the right of the bowl and a fruit-spoon at the left.

A tumbler should be placed at the right of each plate, and a small plate for bread or muffins and butter at the left.

At the right of the two plates there should be a breakfast knife with the edge of the blade towards the plate, a smaller silver knife for butter, and a dessert spoon with bowl turned up to be used for the cereals.

At the left is placed a fork with the tines turned up, and a napkin.

There should be a salt receiver with salt-spoon, and a small pepper-box for the use of every two people at the table. The convenient shake salt is not as generally used as are the small silver and china salt cups.

A waitress should know exactly what food is in preparation for breakfast, and provide her dishes accordingly, seeing that the plates for the meat courses are warm.

Table mats have been discarded by many ladies, and replaced by plain white or hand painted china trays having a narrow rim. These come in a variety of shapes and sizes, and should be placed on the table wherever a hot dish is to be placed.

A side-table will be found very convenient. It should be covered with a table-cloth which can be laundered and may be either plain or elaborately embroidered.

This side table should be large enough to accommodate the muffin plate, the carver and fork, the tablespoons for serving, a tray for serving, a tray for removing whatever is soiled, a small napkin for taking up anything that may be spilled, and a neat white towel to be used for accidental overturning of coffee, milk or water.

On the side board should be placed the ice-water, milk, extra glasses, plates, knives, forks and spoons.

A tray or tray cloth should be placed at the head of the table, where the lady of the house will sit, with the hot water kettle in the centre on its stand beyond her fruit plate. Care should be taken that the lamp is ready to be lighted. The sugar tray with sugar-tongs or spoon, is to be placed at the right of the water kettle and a bowl at the left of it.

At the right of the fruit dish place a china tray or tiles for receiving the coffee pot and hot milk, with small napkin for covering the milk, and place the cups and saucers with spoons at the left of the bread and butter plate.

Just before announcing the breakfast the chairs should be placed at the table, the morning papers where they belong, and all the arrangements quickly reviewed, that nothing may be forgotten.

As soon as the breakfast has been announced, the maid should begin to fill the glasses two-thirds full with water. She will then be ready, with tray in hand, to serve when the family are seated.

In serving the breakfast, the fruit dish should be placed on the tray and offered to each person at the left. If there are guests they should be served first; if there are none, then the lady of the house.

When the fruit course is finished everything pertaining to it should be removed, even though they have not been used.

The maid should take a fruit plate, with finger bowl, knife and spoon in each hand, quickly and quietly to the pantry, removing any spots deftly with the napkin kept for the purpose.

When all are removed the fruit dish should then be taken from the table, and the dish of oatmeal or other cereal preparation brought and placed on the tray at the foot of the table, with a tablespoon at the right of it.

Before each person should then be placed an oatmeal saucer on a plate, and the cover of the dish removed to the side table, the dish placed on the serving tray, the spoon put in the dish, which should then be offered from the left to each person in same order as fruit was served, the cream and sugar passed afterwards.

When the cereal course is finished, the cereal dish with its tray should be placed on the side table and covered, and the maid should then take in each hand a cereal dish and plate to the pantry until all are removed.

Another tray or a tray cloth is then placed at the foot of the table to receive the platter containing the meat or fish, with a small carving knife and tablespoon at the right of the platter and a small carving fork at the left, placing the warm plates in front of the platter.

When the meat or fish has been placed on one

of the plates it should be carried on the tray to the right of each person served, and the maid should herself place it on the table in the order designated by the carver, who asks each one how he shall serve them.

The potato dish should then be taken from the side table and placed, uncovered, upon the tray, and a tablespoon placed in the dish, which should then be served from the left.

The bread plate should then be placed on the table with cold bread, and the muffins passed.

When the coffee is poured, a cup should be taken, as soon as filled, and carried to the one for whom it was intended, and placed by the maid on the table.

A waitress, when not employed in serving, should stand somewhere near the lady of the house, and should be quick to note anything that is needed by the different members of the family, and should be watchful of all parts of the table.

She should instantly refill glasses of water that are emptied, unless carafes are used, and each one is expected to fill his own glass.

A waitress ought not to show by any muscle of the face that she is interested or has taken any note of the conversation at the table.

When the meat course has been served, and the muffins and bread passed, it is generally customary for the maid to leave the dining room in order that she may attend to work in other parts of the house, but, before doing so, she should be quite sure that everything which needs to be done has been finished.

CHAPTER VI.

HOW TO TRAIN A WAITRESS.

LUNCH.

BEFORE the waitress commences to set the table for luncheon, she should air the room for a few minutes, and look about her to see if the room has lost its fresh look since breakfast. It may be necessary to use the dust-cloth again on some of the polished pieces of furniture.

Luncheon, although an informal meal, is, perhaps the most dainty one of the day, and embroidered squares for the centre of the table, and small ones for placing underneath the plates, are exceedingly pretty on a colored table-cloth, especially if it is a pale gray or buff one.

A pot of ferns, placed in one of the vases that come for the purpose of concealing the plain flower-pot, is a pretty decoration for the centre of a lunch table, when cut flowers are not to be obtained. Indeed, any bright, fresh-looking plant that is growing in the windows adds much to the attractiveness of the table.

At the head of the table should be arranged a place for the cocoa pot, with sugar bowl and tongs, teaspoons, cups and saucers.

At the foot of the table a small carving cloth.

If carafes are used, place one at the head and foot of the table at the right side, also salt and pepper between every two people.

Place a luncheon plate for each person, the same size that is used for breakfast. At the right of this, place two knives, with the edges turned towards the plate, a soup spoon if stewed oysters are to be served, and a dessert spoon, two glasses, one for water and the other for milk.

At the left place the small bread and butter plate, a fork with the tines turned up, and a napkin.

Cut some thin slices from the loaf of bread,

and arrange on a bread-plate covered with a small doily, and have the loaf of bread on the bread-plate with the bread-knife, placed on the side-table, so that the slices of bread may be quickly replenished.

Have also on your side-table whatever is likely to be called for, as cheese, powdered sugar, Worcestershire sauce, also have the dessert plates and finger-bowls placed there.

On the side-board have water-pitcher, extra glasses, knives and forks.

See that the platter for the meat or fish to be served is warm, also that the plates are warmed.

A waitress should always take a last look at the table, side-board and side-table to see that everything is in readiness before announcing the luncheon, and should also find out from the mistress if she wishes the meal hastened or delayed beyond the appointed hour.

After it has been announced she should immediately commence to fill the glasses, and be ready with tray in hand to serve whatever is prepared.

If oyster stew, the small oyster dishes should be used and must be warmed, and the waitress can herself serve from the side-table and place one on the plate before each person as they come to the table, serving the crackers from a cracker-plate, which should be placed on the tray with a table-spoon, if the crackers are small, and offered to each person at the left.

To remove the oyster course, take in each hand a plate with the oyster-dish and spoon, and carry to the pantry.

The meat or fish should then be placed on the tray cloth at the foot of the table, with the carver, fork and tablespoon at the right of it, and as it is served the waitress should herself lift the plate with her right hand, and place it on her tray, carry it to each person, the lady of the house first, or the guests if there are any, and place before each one, going to their right.

If potatoes or a vegetable is to be served, it should be taken on a tray, with a spoon in the dish, and offered to each person from their left.

The bread should then be passed and glasses be filled, if needed.

A waitress should keep strict watch that nothing is asked for that is on the table.

In removing this course the carver, fork and knife should be placed on a tray used for this purpose, and carried first to the pantry, then the platter should be removed, then the vegetable dishes, and lastly each person's plate should be taken. The tray-cloth for platters should then be removed, the bread and butter plates and the salt and pepper.

Remove the crumbs with a silver crumb knife and plate, or a napkin may be folded and used for that purpose.

A dessert plate, with fork or spoon and finger bowl, should then be placed before each person, and whatever has been prepared should be passed, either cake or jelly, or a simple dessert dish or fruit. It should be offered at the left of each one. The dish may then be placed before the lady of the house and the cocoa pot brought in and served, the waitress placing the cup at the right of each person.

As lunch ought to be an informal meal the maid is now at liberty to withdraw, after seeing that the glasses are filled, and, if more of the course is desired, the lady of the house serves it, and it is passed at the table.

A waitress is expected to have a general care and oversight of the table linen and a systematic housekeeper will appreciate the advantage of having napkins numbered that are in general use.

For a family of four, one dozen napkins is all that is required for ordinary purposes, when the the napkins are changed twice a week, although it is much more economical to have two dozen in use, as they will wear longer than if each dozen is used separately, because they need not be laundered as frequently.

If more frequent change is made, or if the family is larger, a proportionately greater number will be required.

The numbers from one to four are used the

early part of the week; these are changed in the middle of the week, and from five to eight are taken. While these are being laundered, from nine to twelve are in service, and after that from one to four of the second dozen, and so on.

In this way with the two dozen it will be seen that each napkin is laundered once in three weeks.

If they are not numbered and are placed in the drawer indiscriminately it would not be possible to know just how often each one is in use, and consequently they would not wear evenly; some of the dozen would be threadbare while the others would still be new.

It is an excellent plan to make some difference between those that are given to guests and those which are used ordinarily by the family—either in the marking or by the quality, otherwise the run of the numbers for daily service would be broken and lost if they were given to occasional guests.

CHAPTER VII.

HOW TO TRAIN A WAITRESS.

DINNER.

A FEW cut flowers are often seen at the table, or a growing plant, in families where there is no pretence to elaborate serving. It is a custom which is growing daily, and betokens a refinement independent of wealth or position.

With care, cut flowers can be made to last several days. The waitress should remove them before the table is cleared away, to a cool place, and should see that the water is changed daily.

Dinner is the most ceremonious meal of the day, and more service is required of the maid than at breakfast and supper. She should see that the temperature of the room is right, and in winter should open the windows for a few minutes to freshen the air, and remove, with a soft cloth, any dust that may have gathered since luncheon.

When it is possible, a separate table-cloth should be kept for use at dinner, and, if slightly starched when laundered, it will retain its freshness for a longer time. It should be placed smoothly on the table, over the Canton felting, and care should be taken that it is not in the least askew.

If there are flowers place them on a centre-piece of linen in the middle of the table; if a growing plant, it should be placed either in a flower-vase, large enough to accommodate the pot, or white tissue-paper can be wrapped about the pot to conceal it, or an ornamental cover made of tissue-paper can be slipped on over the pot.

If candelabra are used, place one on either side of the flowers, about half-way between them and the end of the table.

If candlesticks are used, four of them should

be placed to form the corners of a square about the flowers, a little distance from them.

There should be a carving-cloth at the head and one at the foot of the table.

At the right of each person should be placed a soup-spoon, with the bowl turned up, a dinner-knife with the sharp edge turned toward the plate, a fish-knife, if fish is served, and a tumbler for water.

At the left two forks are placed, the smaller one for fish, and a folded napkin within which is a small piece of bread or a dinner-roll.

A dinner plate may also be placed on the table for each person, if preferred. This is often done, as handsome china adds greatly to the appearance, and presents a more pleasing variety than if merely knives, forks, napkins and spoons are first seen.

The dinner-plate can be exchanged by the waitress for the soup-plate, and removed to the side-table, or the soup-plate may be placed on the dinner-plate and removed together when the soup course is changed.

If olives or salted almonds are to be served,

they should be placed in small fancy china or glass dishes, just beyond the candelabra or candlesticks.

If carafes are used, place them at the four corners of the table, or at either end, if two are used. Place a salt-dish and pepper box for the use of every two persons at the table.

On the side-table should be placed the plates that are used for the different courses, the table-spoons, sauce ladles, carvers and forks.

On the sideboard extra glasses, knives, forks and spoons should be arranged; also a tray containing the after-dinner cups and saucers, with a small spoon placed beside each one, a bonbon tray containing cut loaf sugar and tongs, and a small cream-pitcher.

The dessert-plates are also arranged on the sideboard, with a small doily, and a finger-bowl, containing a little warm water, upon each one of them.

The soup-tureen, fish and meat platter, vegetable dishes, gravy dishes and the plates must be placed where they can be heated.

When it is time for dinner the waitress should see that the chairs are placed, should light the candles, fill the carafes and tumblers, place the soup-tureen and warm soup-plates at the head of the table, with the soup-ladle at the right of the tureen, and announce, "The dinner is served."

The soup-tureen should not be uncovered until all are seated. The waitress should then lay the cover on the side-table, and, standing at the left of the hostess, lift each soup-plate as served, place it on her tray, and take it first to the person at the right of the hostess, and serve all on that side first; then begin at the left of the hostess and serve all on that side.

In removing the course, the tureen should be taken to the pantry first, then the soup-plates, one in each hand.

The platter of fish, with the warmed fish-plates, should then be placed on the table, with the fish-knife laid at the right of the platter and the fish-fork at the left. This should be placed at the foot of the table to be served. If there is no gentleman in the family, the person occupying that seat will serve it.

The waitress should, with her right hand, place each plate, as it is served, on her tray, and carry it to the right of the person served, placing it before them, commencing with the one sitting at the right of the server, and continuing on that side, then at the left of the server, and to all on that side.

The sauce-dish, with ladle, should then be passed on the tray and offered at the left of each person.

Small thin pieces of bread, or rolls, may then be passed.

In removing the fish course, the fish platter should be taken first, then the sauce-dish, then the plates, one in each hand, until all are taken to the pantry.

The meat should then be placed before the carver, together with the warmed plates, a carving-knife and spoon at the right of the platter and the carving-fork at the left of it. The vegetables should be placed on the side-table.

While the meat is being carved, if there are almonds and olives on the table they are placed on the tray and offered at the left of each person.

The roast should then be served in the same manner as the fish, and if there is gravy it should be served the same as the fish-sauce.

A spoon should be placed in the potato-dish, and the potatoes offered at the left of each person, the potato-dish to be returned to the side-table.

Other vegetables to be served in the same way, and returned to the table.

In removing this course, the carver, carving-fork and gravy-spoon should be placed on a waiter which has no napkin on it, and carried to the pantry; then the platter with the meat should be taken, the gravy-dish with ladle, and the plates, one in each hand; also the vegetable dishes removed from the side-table.

Crumbs should then be brushed from the table-cloth by means of a silver crumb-knife and plate, or a fresh napkin, neatly folded, will answer the same purpose as the silver knife.

If a salad course is to be served, place the salad-bowl and salad-plate before the lady of the house. If it is lettuce, and the French dressing is to be prepared at the table, place the oil, vinegar, mustard, salt and pepper, before her, together with a mixing-spoon and fork.

If the salad is already dressed, the salad-fork and spoon should be placed in the salad-bowl, and a clean knife and fork at each place—this must be done quickly and quietly.

As the salad is served, it should be taken first to the person at the right of the server, and placed there, then to all on that side, and, after they are served, to those on the left side.

If crackers and cheese are served with the salad, they should then be offered on the tray to the left of each person.

In removing the course the salad-bowl is taken, then the salad-plates, the oil, vinegar, pepper, salt-boxes, olives and almonds.

Remove the crumbs again, then the carving-cloths, leaving nothing on the table except flowers or candles.

A dessert-plate, with finger-bowl and dessert-fork, should then be placed before each person, and the dish containing the dessert before the lady of the house, together with knife, fork or spoon for serving. This should be taken in the same way, first to all those on the right side, and then on the left.

To remove this course, take first the dessert and whatever was used for serving it, then the plates and finger-bowls.

If coffee is to be served at the table, and not in the drawing room, the tray containing the service may be placed before the lady of the house, together with the coffee-pot or urn; or it may be removed to the pantry, the waitress filling the cups about two-thirds full, and then placing one at the right of each person and offering cut loaf sugar and cream on a smaller tray at the left of each one.

After the coffee is served, the waitress should await the signal from her mistress to withdraw, previously noting if the carafes need to be replenished.

If carafes are not used, she must be carefully observant, throughout the meal, to replenish glasses immediately when needed.

There should be no conversation with a waitress at the table, and one who is thoroughly well trained understands that she is to keep an observant watch, that she may anticipate all wants without the necessity of making them known.

A waitress should not commence to remove a course until every person at the table has finished with it.

The directions for serving are generally not arbitrary rules, because customs often vary with locality, and in many cases individual characteristics are as marked in table serving and table adornments as in the furnishing of the rooms.

CHAPTER VIII.

HOW TO TRAIN A WAITRESS.

CHAMBER WORK AND FRONT DOOR SERVICE.

THE duties of a waitress or second girl are by no means confined to table serving and the dining-room.

In a small family where a cook and waitress are employed, it is usually expected that they perform the entire work of the household without assistance of the mistress, beyond a general superintendence. Just how this work shall be divided is a point which must be settled by circumstances and the individual needs of the family.

In no two households, perhaps, is there a like distribution, but there are certain general duties which are incumbent upon a waitress, wherever one is employed, and, among these, chamber service is by no means the least important.

The maid, after having served the meat course at breakfast, should be given to understand that she is at liberty to leave the dining-room, and this will be her opportunity for going through each bed-room, removing the slops, washing and wiping the different articles of the toilet set belonging to the washstands, refilling pitchers, removing soiled towels and replacing them with fresh ones.

It is presumed that the occupants of bedrooms will have taken the clothing from the beds, and placed it to air near an open window, if the day is pleasant, before leaving their rooms.

There can hardly be too much air and sunshine in bedrooms when the beds are not occupied.

They should be stripped of their clothing in the morning, the mattress thrown across the foot of the bed, that the air may circulate freely through the under side, and so left until thoroughly aired. It is not the best housekeepers who have their beds made as soon as the sleepers are out of them.

Night dresses should be as thoroughly aired as the bed clothing, and through the day should be hung up in a closet or elsewhere, and not folded up and placed under the pillows.

Particular attention should be given to the toothbrush-holder and mug, and the attention of the maid should be called to the necessity of emptying out all the water that is left in the pitchers before filling them afresh. Unless this is spoken of, there are few maids who will take the trouble to do so. Water which stands in a bedroom absorbs impurities.

Many housekeepers require that the water that has stood in the pitchers during the day shall be replaced with fresh water just before retiring.

A heavy china or crockery slop-jar is far preferable to a tin one.

They should be thoroughly scalded and dried each morning, and once or twice a week hot water that has a teaspoonful of soda dissolved in it should stand in the pails for an hour.

Each bed should be allowed to air for at least

one hour, and during that time the bed-rooms may be dusted, threads and lint removed from the carpet, and the room made tidy.

If the mattress is made in two pieces it can be easily turned, and should be daily. Once a week it ought to be brushed thoroughly on both sides with a whisk broom, in order to prevent dust from accumulating in the tackings.

As often as once a week pillows and blankets should be placed on the clothes-line and allowed to remain an hour or two in the fresh air ; the pillows must be kept out of the sun. This should be done in the morning when the sun is shining brightly, which will prevent their gathering dampness.

In making a bed, care should be taken that the under sheet is placed smoothly over the mattress and tucked firmly under it on all sides : that the open end of the blankets should be placed at the head of the bed, and, if two people are to occupy a bed, place one pair of blankets sidewise and one pair lengthwise of the bed.

Definite instructions should be given a new maid as to just how to arrange a room and bed for the day and night.

If there are guests in the house, the work in the guest-chamber should be attended to first.

Just before retiring at night, the maid should be instructed to go through the different bedrooms removing shams and spreads, folding the latter carefully. She should turn down the upper sheet and clothing, placing the pillows in position for use; should lay the nightdress on the bed, and arrange an extra covering at the foot of the bed in such a way that it may be conveniently at hand, if needed, during the night. All waste water should be removed, and fresh drinking water brought. A glass water-bottle or carafe, with tumbler fitting over the neck, is of great service in a chamber or sick room.

If there are guests in the house the maid should knock at their door with a pitcher of hot water early enough in the morning to allow them sufficient time for dressing.

THE FRONT DOOR.

Some one has said that the manner and appearance of a maid at the front door in answer to the bell is the key-note of the establishment. It cannot be denied that it is important, and special instruction upon this point should be given.

A fresh white apron should be placed conveniently near during the hours of morning work where it can be put on at a moment's notice if the bell rings, the same apron to be used for serving at the table.

The ring should always be answered as promptly as possible, and the door opened sufficiently to suggest a welcome, the maid to be plainly visible, and under no circumstances to remain partially concealed behind the door, with head appearing from the side, or arm thrust out to receive a card.

A maid should understand that a certain amount of care and civility is expected of her in this service, and a mistress should be as explicit as possible in regard to instruction, as it is the one thing that she cannot personally superintend.

A small tray for receiving cards and notes should be provided to be placed conveniently near the door, so that in passing the waitress may take it in her hand and hold it by her side, partially concealed among the folds of her dress. In case the visitor gives her name instead of her card, care should be taken that the tray is not visible, in order that she may not feel she has neglected a courtesy expected of her. On the other hand, it is a pleasure to find a maid prepared to receive a card as soon as it is presented, without the delay of reaching for the tray, however near at hand it may be.

If a mistress is indisposed or has any engagement which will prevent her from receiving calls the maid should be instructed to that effect, before going to the door.

A conscientious mistress will not instruct a maid to say "not at home" when she is in the house, because, although the phrase may be for her sufficiently conventional to reconcile her to its use, it may not be for the maid.

If it simply means that one is engaged, or not receiving, why not say so? It is as good form as the other phrase, and is a much more honest and safe one to use.

While a certain graciousness of manner is pleasant from the maid, care should be taken that she is not too friendly with callers, or does not volunteer unnecessary information.

In showing a guest out, the waitress should open the door wide, holding it so until the guest has descended the steps, or perhaps has gained the street, if it is a short walk. She should then close it so softly that it may not be heard.

Caution should be given the waitress in regard to admitting agents into the house. Many, claiming to be such, simply take that means for gaining access, and often, cases of theft have been the result of carelessness of the maid in admitting them.

CHAPTER IX.

THE RANGE AND FUEL.

NEARLY all rented houses in cities are supplied with either a set range or a portable one. It should be ascertained if it is in good condition before taking possession, as much of the comfort of the family will depend upon whether the food is well cooked.

If you must supply a range or stove inform yourself in regard to the different makes in the market, and select the best one you can find, with a plain finish that may be easily kept clean.

Be sure that the dampers and doors will shut closely, as this is necessary for controlling the heat.

Ranges are more generally used than stoves,

for the reason that they can be set nearer to the wall and will take up less room in the kitchen. The difference is that stoves have doors on both sides of the oven instead of one side.

A housekeeper should understand thoroughly the mechanism of her stove, how to make and keep a fire, how to regulate it, and to learn the hottest and coolest places in the oven. She should make sure that her servant understands also, and should personally superintend the cooking until satisfied on these points.

Whatever is placed in the oven will need a certain amount of watching, at first, to see if it is baking too fast or too slowly. If too fast, and the dampers are closed, a cover may be lifted from the top of the stove for a minute or two, or a piece of stiff brown paper placed to screen whatever is baking from the direct heat. Or a pan of water placed in the oven will often cool it.

When the oven is not hot enough the ashes should be raked from the grate, and the dampers opened in order to have a direct draught.

When the fire is not needed for cooking or other purposes, the draughts should be closed, that the fuel may not be wasted, and this is a point that it is almost impossible to carry out with the average maid, and it will require much firmness and patience in the mistress.

When making a fire the covers should be taken off and the soot first brushed off from the top of the oven into the grate. This should be done every morning and not occasionally as is often the case.

Turn the grate over until free from cinders and ashes, remove these to a coal-sifter placed over an iron ash barrel, and place the cinders when sifted in a receptacle kept for that purpose—they can be frequently used on a furnace fire, and occasionally will answer for the range.

A loose roll of paper is first placed on the grate, and on this some small pine kindlings crossed over each other that the air may circulate freely through them. Care must be taken that the wood comes out to each end of the fire box.

Over this it is a good idea to cross two sticks of hard wood if you have it, as that will burn longer than the soft wood and assist the coal to catch.

If kindling wood alone is used it will be necessary to use more wood than if the hard wood is put with it.

The stove should be blacked before the fire is lighted—this can be done with a good stove polish dissolved in a little water, and applied with a painter's brush, to be rubbed in and polished afterwards with a dry stove brush. The blacking should be thoroughly rubbed in at this time or it will come off whenever the stove is brushed afterwards, and if the fire is started, after it is rubbed in, it will polish more easily.

Many good housekeepers are discarding stove polish, and in its stead are using olive oil which is rubbed into the stove every morning when it is cold.

In this way the stove is kept black, and although its surface is not polished, it is cleaner than it is if the lead is used and whatever is spilled on it, can be easily removed with soap and water.

After the process of cleaning the stove is finished, open the dampers and light the paper. When the wood is burning freely, put the coal in, taking care that it does not come above the point where a supply of air can penetrate through the fuel.

Most servants are especially obtuse on this point, and insist upon filling the stove even to the covers. By so doing almost twice the amount of coal necessary to produce the same amount of heat is used.

After the fire is made, only a small quantity of coal should be fed at a time, and this should be distributed evenly over the surface—as a large amount will lower the temperature so that it will not be available for use until all the fresh coal has become ignited.

If the top of the oven and the grate at the bottom is kept free from ashes, much less fuel will be needed. Oxygen is as necessary as fuel in keeping a fire, and anything that prevents free access of oxygen through the fuel, prevents perfect combustion.

Fuel is an important item in household expenses, and it is often surprising to find how little some housekeepers know about the respective qualities of red ash and white ash coal.

In many country towns, wood is burned almost entirely, and housekeepers who are accustomed to its use prefer it to coal, as it is cleaner, and more easily managed — but it is much more expensive than coal.

In many of the smaller cities and larger towns white ash coal is, frequently, the only variety that can be obtained. For range use, however, a good red ash coal gives out more heat, and is more economical than any other variety.

The cook does not like it as well, especially if she is not an early riser, because it does not burn up as rapidly as white ash, and cannot be started as quickly, but when it is thoroughly ignited, its lasting powers are surprising.

Another variety of coal called the "Franklin" is a softer coal, and burns more freely even than the white ash. A fire can be started very quickly with this coal, and it is to be recommended in cases when the chimney does not draw well.

It is necessary, however, to keep constant watch of the dampers in the stove or range, if the winter's supply of coal is expected to last as long as it should.

Perhaps the cheapest fuel that can be used for cooking is kerosene oil, and the stoves for burning the oil have been so perfected that the entire cooking for a family may be performed on them —but they require even more care to perform satisfactory work than the ordinary range.

Unless they are properly cleaned the odor from them is very objectionable. The netting and open space under the burners should be kept open and free from soot, and the burners should be frequently cleaned and scoured with sapolio, or kitchen mineral soap and water.

There should be no brown deposit allowed to remain on them—whatever can not be scoured off, should be scraped off with a knife, and the charred part of the wick rubbed off.

When the stove is not in use, the wicks should be turned down, and the oil wiped from the burners. This is an important point, because if allowed to accumulate, it will harden on the burner and be difficult to remove, and the odor from it will be worse every time it is used.

CHAPTER X.

WASHING.

MONDAY has been selected as a general washing day by housekeepers all over the land; but it is open to objection, since it involves much preparation, and labor of assorting and soaking the clothes either Saturday or Sunday evening.

If Sunday evening is taken for this purpose it is an infringement of the day that few conscientious people care to make. If Saturday, the table linen must be changed that day in order that it may be looked over with a view to removing stains or darning rents, and we lose the fresh look that is to be desired for our Sunday meals.

The change of undergarments is also necessitated, and if these need to be mended before they are washed, Saturday is not always the best day for that purpose, as with many of us it is a busy day, and with others partakes more of the nature of a holiday, than perhaps any other week day. In very warm weather it is not quite safe to leave clothes soaking in water from Saturday night until Monday morning. Tuesday as a washing day is not open to the same objections, as it gives ample time on Monday for the sorting and darning process, although in case the weather is not propitious for a good "drying day," the ironing is delayed until the latter part of the week, and the system of work disarranged. Every housewife must settle for herself which is the lesser of the two evils.

It is always a matter of regret when the kitchen must be used for a laundry, as the effluvia which rises from the washing of soiled clothes is an objectionable thing in a cooking room.

To insure satisfactory work, good water and good soap are necessities. If the water is hard it should be softened by the use of ammonia or borax.

In purchasing soap for laundry use, the wisest plan is to get a box at a time. It is cheaper and the soap spends better if put away to dry before using.

Stains and grease spots should be removed from all articles before they are washed.

Ink spots may be removed from cotton or linen goods with tartaric acid; wet the article and drop the acid on the spot, letting it remain in strong sunlight for a time, then wash it out in cold water.

To remove grass stains, rub them thoroughly with molasses, and then rinse in clear water, and repeat the process till the stain disappears, or wet the stain and rub it freely with soap and baking soda and let it lie a short time before washing.

Fruit stains can usually be removed by pouring boiling rain water through them and repeating the process several times if they are obstinate. Be sure that soap or soap suds is not used on them.

Pear stains are more difficult to remove than those made by grapes or berries. Powdered starch is sometimes sprinkled over the stains, and the boiling water poured on it. Tea and coffee stains may be removed by means of hot water to which a little borax has been added.

Fresh paint can be removed with turpentine.

To remove mildew from cotton or linen, wet the fabric in soap suds and spread it on a dish, or on the grass in the sun. Then take equal quantities of pulverized chalk and soft soap and spread this over the mildew. The sun, if it is a hot day, will usually remove it. If it does not do so readily, put the cloth in soap suds over night, and repeat the chalk and soap every morning, until the mildew is gone. Another way is to soak the spots in buttermilk and spread on the grass in a strong sunshine.

Wheel grease on wash dresses can be removed by wetting it first with kerosene, and then washing it with soap and warm water.

Blood stains should be soaked and washed in

clear cold water first, then soaped freely and allowed to soak again over night.

After all spots have been removed, all the finer articles should be sorted out for the washing first, and should be placed by themselves in a tub of lukewarm water with a little soap. Add some powdered borax or a little ammonia if the water is not soft.

Place the coarse clothes in another tub and rub the soiled parts well with soap. A little powdered borax or ammonia should be added to this water also.

Soak them over night, and the next morning pass them through a wringer into another tub of hot suds. Rub them thoroughly on a zinc-faced washing board which is less liable to wear the clothes than a wooden one, and then put them into a boiler of cold water containing a small piece of soap. Let them boil three or four minutes after they reach the boiling point, and then drain them into a tub of cold water, and wring them from this into a tub of lukewarm water to which has been added a little bluing.

After wringing from this water, separate what ever can be starched before it is dried, from the rest of the clothes, which may be hung out to dry immediately.

Spread a clean cloth in your clothes basket before putting in the clothes that are to be hung out.

A galvanized wire clothes line is better than rope, as it need not be taken down and is always ready for use, and a clothes pin apron for holding the clothes pins is much more convenient than a basket as it admits a free use of the hands.

This is made from a piece of bed-ticking for the foundation 21 inches wide and 14 inches deep, or of any material that is strong. Over this place another piece of the material of the size as the first, cutting off the corners of the upper part of this second piece to form the openings in the pocket for taking out the clothes pins.

Bind around the edges with braid, gather the fullness at the top and sew to a binding. Tack tapes to either end for tying about the waist and for hanging it up by when not in use.

If your wash day happens to be rainy, and you do not care to postpone, all the white clothes except the flannels may be washed, and left to soak in the rinsing water.

Wring them out the next day, pass them through the bluing water, and hang them out. They will often look whiter for the delay.

To wash flannels, do not put them into water more than blood warm, and never boil them. Sufficient ammonia to make the water feel slippery is of great advantage in washing white flannels, and will be of assistance in making a strong suds. Flannels must not be put to soak, and the soap must not be rubbed on them.

Knead them in the water something as you knead bread, pressing the dirt out of them as much as possible.

If they are much soiled, prepare a second water in the same way with ammonia and make a strong suds.

Rinse them quickly in two waters, wring them as dry as possible through the wringer, shake out well and hang up immediately, for if they are allowed to remain for a long time in the clothes basket they will shrink.

Flannels ought to be washed early in the day in warm weather, and should be dried thoroughly, as quickly as possible. In winter a clear bright day is of great advantage, and the middle of the day is the best time for putting them out.

To wash colored flannels stir three scant table-spoonfuls of flour into a quart of cold water, and let it boil eight minutes, add this to some clear warm suds, and wash by kneading and pressing them in this. Rinse in three waters, warm water, but not hot.

It is well to have flannels brought in and pressed the same day.

Do not fold them over night. If not convenient to iron the same day, hang smoothly on an inside line or clothes bar, and iron early the next day.

Fine all wool goods are not easily kept from shrinking. Those that have a mixture of cotton are more easily managed. Ammonia should never be used with colored flannels, as it tends to make the colors dull.

Silk underwear should be washed quickly, with white Castile soap, in warm water, softened either with ammonia or borax. They should be thoroughly rinsed in three waters, wrung as dry as possible, and pressed out before thoroughly dry.

For washing colored woolen dress goods use soap bark instead of soap. It can be purchased at any druggist's. It does the work well, and gives a little body to the material such as new goods have.

Soak about ten cents' worth in a pail of warm water over night, then add two-thirds of it to the water in which the goods are to be washed. Wash thoroughly and rinse in warm water, adding the remaining solution of soap bark. Dry rapidly in the open sunshine, and when nearly dry, iron on the wrong side.

Blankets that are in constant use should be washed once a year. If they are to be packed away during the summer, they should be washed on a clear sunshiny spring day.

For light summer blankets that are to be packed away during the winter, a clear bright day in the fall should be chosen.

Not more than two pair of double blankets can be washed satisfactorily at a time and three tubs will be needed for this purpose.

The water should be warm, and sufficient ammonia should be added to make it feel soft and slippery in the hands.

Dissolve in this some shavings of hard white soap until a good suds is formed. Into this place the blankets. Knead them in the water as you do flannels, pressing the water out of them as much as possible, lifting them up and down and squeezing them in the suds.

Wring them into another tub of water of the same temperature, which has also been made slippery with ammonia,—continue the same process in this tub without the soap, and wring them into a third tub of clear water without ammonia, though of the same temperature as the other two.

When wrung from this tub it will require two persons to adjust and hang them on the line.

The corners should be taken in the hands one person to stand at one end, and the other opposite, as far apart from each other as the entire length of the double blanket, which should then be snapped up and down for two or three minutes in the open air, in order to raise the nap of the wool and render it soft and light.

They should then be stretched evenly over the lines, and pulled into shape that they may dry in straight lines. Blankets washed in this way will not full and will look almost as well as when they are new.

White lace curtains and those of thin material should be washed in soft water in which Castile soap has been dissolved. If the water is hard add a little ammonia, not quite as much as for blankets and wash them the same as blankets.

Choose a warm sunny day in the spring for this purpose, and if you have a nicely-kept and well-cut lawn, place the two curtains belonging to the same window together, and stretch on the lawn, pinning them into shape with hairpins stuck through them into the ground.

If you have no lawn, place a sheet on the floor of a room, stretch and pin the two curtains to shape over this, and open all the windows wide that they may dry quickly.

There are many houskeepers who claim to make lighter work of the family washing than by following the directions that have been given.

This is done by means of washing machines, some of which are excellent. Many use a washing fluid which is added to a boiler of clothes in the proportion of one tea cup full of the fluid to the water, which must be cold. Soap is added to this, and the clothes are then put in dry and are taken out just when they come to a boiling point. They are then rubbed through one water, rinsed and placed into the bluing water.

Those who follow this process claim that the fluid saves much of the work of rubbing which is the most tiresome part.

It would be an easy matter for one to try this method and decide for herself if it is more satisfactory. Conservative housekeepers claim that the fluid injures the clothes more than vigorous rubbing.

The following is an excellent rule for making the

WASHING FLUID.

One pound sal soda, one half-pound unslackened lime, a piece of borax the size of an egg, add one gallon of water, and let it come to a boil. Remove from the fire and after it has settled, pour off the clear liquid into a jug or bottles.

CHAPTER XI.

STARCHING, SPRINKLING AND FOLDING.

THE best quality of starch should be used for all clothes. Flour starch which is sometimes used for coarse goods is liable to give a yellow hue which it is difficult to wash out.

Clothes which are first dried, will take the starch better, than if placed into it when wet, but this is a longer process and involves more work and is only necessary for shirt bosoms, cuffs and collars which require to be very stiff.

A housekeeper should have a rule for the making of her starch, and should follow it exactly. Almost every laundress has a way of her own for making clear boiled starch, and her own opinion as to what will make it iron without sticking.

An excellent rule is to dissolve in a saucepan

two tablespoonfuls of starch in a little cold water until it is free from lumps. Upon this pour gradually one quart of boiling water, stirring well all the time until the opaque white of the mixture becomes semi-transparent, and the starch is of a jelly-like subtance.

Let this boil for about five minutes, stirring it during that time. Then stir into this one teaspoonful of kerosene oil, or a tablespoonful of gum arabic water made by dissolving two ounces of pulverized gum arabic in a pint of boiling water — straining this through a piece of cheese cloth, and bottling it while warm. The gum arabic water should be closely corked to prevent it from souring.

The kerosene oil is a simple and inexpensive addition, which will insure a good finish and prevent it from sticking — but the gum arabic will give a higher polish.

If a plain dead finish is desired neither kerosene or gum arabic should be used—in place of this half a teaspoonful of borax may be added.

Shirt bosoms, cuffs and collars, should be thoroughly dried and then coated on both sides with the starch, which must be well rubbed in, and clapped between the hands, that every fibre may be saturated.

Wring until nearly dry, and hang where it will be free from dust, and in cold weather where it will not freeze. When dry, a second starching with cold starch is necessary to attain the desired stiffness.

This is made by dissolving in a cupful of lukewarm water, a teaspoonful of starch—keep the starch well stirred up, and dip the articles into this, put the starched parts together and roll them up in a towel.

Boiled starch may be thinned with hot water for those articles which require but little stiffening.

When the clothes are ready to be taken from the line, fold them smoothly, that no unnecessary creases are made and do not crowd them into the basket.

When ready to be sprinkled, they should be turned right side out, and if they are to be ironed the same day, lukewarm water should be used, but if they can lay over night, cold water will answer as well. They will usually iron better if left over night.

After they are dampened fold each garment smoothly, turning all hems and selvages towards the centre, and roll them very tightly to remove the heavy creases that the wringer is apt to leave.

Starched clothes should be sprinkled but a short time before ironing — as they dry quickly. Shirts and collars need not lie more than an hour. Place them in the clothes basket with a clean cloth under them, and spread a thick blanket over the top of it, and tuck it in at the sides that the air may not dry them.

And just here I would say to those overworked and tired housekeepers, who for economy must do their work without assistance, that it would be more profitable for them to fold as smoothly as possible without ironing, their sheets, rollers and dish towels, work aprons, and the night dresses and night shirts in common wear. Stockings, undervests and drawers can be pulled into shape and look as well as if they were ironed, and both woollen and cotton woven underwear have a more delicate odor if left rough dry.

The time that is saved in this way on ironing days, may be much more profitably spent in reading, rest or recreation.

It is wisdom to know just what can be slighted without detriment to the home.

CHAPTER XII.

IRONING.

PERHAPS there is no household duty which gives more satisfaction to a housewife than the sight of a clothes frame of well ironed clothes.

To insure this it is necessary that the flat irons be perfectly clean and smooth, and that there be sand paper, heavy wrapping paper, cloths, a case knife and a bit of wax encased in a piece of cloth, near at hand for keeping them so during the process.

Neglect and carelessness will render flat irons unfit for use in a short time, while those which are well kept will be equally serviceable after years of constant use.

They should be washed once a month in soap suds with a little ammonia, wiped, and placed on the back of the stove to be thoroughly dried. They should be washed oftener, if the family is large and there are many starched clothes to be done up every week. Keep them when not in use in a closed dry place—as they gather dust if kept on a shelf or mantel.

See that the top of the range is perfectly clean before putting on the irons. With many ranges there is a piece made to set on the top of the stove to accommodate the irons, the covers and centrepiece of the stove to be removed. This piece is made thin, that the irons may heat more quickly and with less fuel. When this is not to be obtained a long griddle made for frying cakes that will fit in the same way, answers the purpose.

Ironing holders should be made sufficiently large to protect the hands well, of some heavy cotton material with an interlining which is pliable.

The irons which come in sets of three, with an adjustable handle, do not need the holders, and are generally liked by housekeepers.

If possible do not allow your irons to become

too hot—if it should happen, cool them by setting on end on the hearth, and never plunge them into cold water, as that will harm the temper of the iron. They should not be kept on the stove when not in use. If starch sticks to the iron always scrape it off with a knife before placing it on the stove to heat. The ironing cloth may be made of heavy felt that comes for the purpose, and should be large enough to cover the table, and pin around each corner, that it may remain smooth and immovable during the ironing—over this should be placed the ironing sheet which should also be pinned at the corners. There should be three of these sheets kept ready for use, changed and laundered as often as necessary.

Skirt boards are now made with standards that can be adjusted to any height, a great improvement over the old method of placing them on chairs. One of them will be necessary for laundry work, also a bosom board; these to be covered with the ironing felt and with cotton, which should be lightly tacked on the under side that it may be easily removed.

The clothes should be ironed until dry. If they are left wet, they will wrinkle as they dry, and much of the smooth, glossy effect will be lost.

Napkins and table cloths will look better if there is a faint trace of starch in them—they need to be thoroughly ironed in every part — to be folded evenly, avoiding in the table cloths as many creases as possible. The ironing of the table linen deserves especial care and attention to render it smooth and glossy, and will amply repay one for the labor expended on it.

To iron sheets,double them smoothly both ways being careful to bring the edges close together, and iron one side thoroughly—turn and fold again on the other side, ironing both sides.

Ginghams and prints are better ironed on the wrong side.

For shirts, iron all the body first before the starched parts. For the bosom, wring a cloth out of cold water, and rub carefully the starched surface as you iron it to remove the particles of starch, which would otherwise adhere to the iron.

Use a moderately hot iron, and pass it carefully and slowly over the surface at first, then slightly moisten the surface again with your wet cloth, and rub hard and quickly, to give a gloss.

Cuffs and collars are first ironed on the wrong side, and then finished on the right—the same caution for removing the particles of starch with a wet cloth should be observed. A good gloss can only be given by using strength, aided by the small polishing iron which comes for the purpose.

But with the utmost care and attention, it is not possible to make them look as they do at a regular laundry, and many prefer to send them there, and save the time and strength expended upon them for other parts of the work.

All ironed clothes should be hung on a clothes-frame until thoroughly dry—a matter to which it would be well if housewives gave more attention. It is of great assistance if the clothes which need mending are, when ironed, placed on a separate bar.

CHAPTER XIII.

SWEEPING AND DUSTING.

IT would seem that everybody who is old enough to be a housekeeper ought to know how to sweep and dust a room satisfactorily but there are many women who, not having had the practical experience on this point necessary to insure good results, are not in a position to insist upon thorough work in this direction from the maid.

The preparation of the room and the arrangement of the furniture and other articles after it has been cleaned are more work than the mere sweeping and dusting.

Bric-a-brac and fancy articles should be dusted or wiped carefully and removed to another room. Soft cheese cloth, or a silk handkerchief makes an excellent dust cloth.

Pieces of furniture and chairs which are easily

moved should be dusted and placed in an adjoining room.

Stuffed furniture should be beaten when it is possible with a rattan beater, the dust from the folds and tuftings removed with a pointed brush, that comes for the purpose, resembling a painter's brush, and the surface then carefully brushed with a hand broom. Large pieces of furniture that can not be removed should be carefully and closely covered with dusting sheets.

In sweeping bed rooms, the bed should first be dusted, then made and covered over with a large sweeping cloth.

Rugs should be swept and placed over the clothes lines out doors for the air to freshen.

Portieres should be unhooked from the rings, brushed and shaken out doors.

Muslin or lace draperies at the windows should be lifted and removed with the pole from the supporting brackets, and the dust brushed or shaken from them.

The windows should be opened and the blinds

dusted. If the windows need washing this should not be done until after the sweeping, when the paint is wiped.

Cover the broom with a soft cloth, and brush the walls, cornice, ceilings, tops of doors and windows, or use a long feather duster for the purpose.

Dust the pictures and cover them over with cloths.

A Brussels or nap carpet should be swept with short, light, even strokes, with the grain for the first stroke, then across it for the next, and so on over the carpet, brushing around the edges and in the corners with a whisk broom. To sweep a room without raising a dust, scatter dampened bits of paper over the carpet.

After sweeping the room, the dust should be allowed to settle for five or ten minutes, then dampen your broom and go over the carpet lightly, which will remove all the dust, after which it may be wiped up with a damp cloth, which has been wrung out as dry as possible from water to which a few drops of ammonia have been added.

The closets should be swept, and the floor wiped with a wet cloth, and the door left open to air awhile every sweeping day.

Before replacing the furniture, wipe off all finger marks and spots from the woodwork, polish the mirrors, and if there is a fireplace the hearth should be washed up, the iron work rubbed off with a rag dampened slightly with kerosene, and the brasses polished, after which the dusting sheets may be removed, and the furniture replaced.

Such a sweeping should be a part of the regular housework every week, for rooms that are carpeted and used constantly, in order to ensure health and cleanliness.

It is better to set apart one day for a sweeping day, as for washing and ironing.

It is a convenience to have a separate broom, brush broom and dust pan for upstairs work—and another set for the rooms downstairs.

The broom used for the kitchen should be kept for that purpose, and not used on the carpets, and a separate broom should be kept for the cellar which needs to be swept and brushed down once a week.

Halls and rooms that are not carpeted are better swept with a long handled brush broom that takes up the dirt and dust easily, and does not scratch the polished surface. Such rooms need to be swept once a day.

It is an excellent plan to have two bags made of white cotton flannel for slipping over a broom. If, after sweeping, the polished or painted floor is brushed over with this, it will remove all dust; the bags to be laundered alternately each week.

For sweeping stairs that are carpeted, a stiff whisk broom is needed. The dirt should be swept from each step into the dust pan, and not from one step to the other. A painter's brush is excellent for sweeping the dirt from the corners.

For furniture covers cheap unbleached cotton cloth is excellent—the seams can be stitched together on the machine, and three breadths are needed for each cover. They should be from three to three and a half yards in length. Six of these are sufficient for the needs of a household.

CHAPTER XIV.

DISHWASHING. CARE OF THE SINK.

ALL dishes should be well scraped before they are washed, and it is advisable to have a small wooden knife for this purpose.

A dish mop is excellent for cups and the cleanest dishes, but there is nothing better than soft linen crash cut of convenient size, hemmed, and with a loop of tape tacked to it for hanging it up by.

There should be six of these dishcloths, and a fresh one should be substituted every week and the one in use put into the weekly wash to be boiled and ironed. It is well to number these dish cloths, that they may be used in regular rotation.

To those who have been in the habit of using

parts of worn articles of table linen or of clothing for this purpose it will doubtless seem extravagant to purchase new material, but it will be found to do better work, and is more easily kept clean, which is a most important item from a sanitary point of view.

A celebrated physician has said that a dish cloth left without washing, in a lump over night, will ferment and generate germs of disease for any one whose breathing apparatus is brought into direct contact with them.

Ragged or linty dish cloths should not be used for the reason that lint will collect in the sink spout, and may cause a serious obstruction.

Besides these linen cloths, a chain dish cloth for kettles, frypans, etc., made of wire rings is of great assistance in removing whatever is burned on in cooking.

For dish towels there is nothing better than the glass towelling of linen, barred with blue or red. It wears well, and leaves no lint on the dishes, and is quite as economical as the best quality of crash.

Dish towels are too often made of coarse harsh linen which when new will not wipe the dishes dry, and after it has become old, it is apt to retain a greasy smell.

Do not use towels that are part cotton, for they will not do the work well.

After every dish-washing the dish cloth and towels should be thoroughly washed and placed where they will dry quickly. A rod attached to the stove is used for the purpose. As often as the weather permits they should be dried out doors. In every household it ought to be a rule that the towels and dish cloths be put into the wash once a week, and a fresh supply used. Those that are washed should be inspected by the mistress, and not left in the kitchen.

There should always be two pans for washing dishes, one to contain hot suds in which they are washed and the other clear hot dish water in which they are rinsed. There is a convenient little article for holding soap, made of open wires which permits the use of small pieces. This is placed in the hot water and shaken about, and will produce suds quickly, especially if a few drops of household ammonia have been added to the water.

The water in the pan for washing dishes should be changed frequently. Do not allow it to deposit a greasy rim around the pan above the edge of the water.

A rack for draining dishes is a convenience; this is made of open wires.

If there is a butler's pantry, the china, silver and glass ware should be washed there. If there is no butler's pantry, and no room or convenience for washing them in the china closet, an ordinary table in the kitchen may be used for the purpose, placed as near the slide as possible. It lessens the tendency to accidents in dish breaking, not to have them carried to the kitchen sink. Boiling water should never be poured over fine china, as it is apt to injure the glaze and in course of time will show tiny lines of crackle over it.

China and glass ware should not be washed in water that is too hot for the hands.

The glasses should be washed first, then the silver, cups and saucers, and lastly the dishes.

Do not allow too many to accumulate before wiping them.

Do not place ivory or bone handled knives into the dish pan or the blades into a pitcher containing hot water, as many do. The sudden expansion of the steel by the heat will often cause the handles to crack. Wash them thoroughly out of the water with the dish cloth, and wipe them dry.

The more common dishes, and those used for cooking and the ironware and tinware are washed in the sink.

Wash all the ironware outside as well as inside, in hot soapy water, rinse in clean hot water and wipe dry.

Coarse soft linen towels are used for this purpose and for the common dishes.

Greasy pans, and fry kettles, can be more easily washed if a teaspoonful of soda is added to the water.

Sapolio, and kitchen mineral soap will remove whatever has been burnt on in cooking. If you wash meat pans and greasy pots and kettles as soon as they are emptied, you will save yourself much trouble. If you cannot wash them at once fill them with hot water.

Always keep the inside of the coffee pot bright to insure good coffee. Boil it out occasionally with soap water and wood ashes and scour thoroughly.

Do not let a Dover egg beater soak in water when it has been used, because the oil will be taken out from the gears and the beater will be hard to turn. The wires should be wiped as soon as they are used, with a damp cloth, and it should be kept well oiled.

Before putting the dish pans away, scald thoroughly, making sure that no grease remains on them, and wipe until quite dry.

A fine strainer pan is almost a necessity in a sink, and through it, all dish water, and liquid refuse ought to be poured, and the scraps and crumbs remaining in the strainer, can either be burned or placed in the refuse pail.

When every precaution has been taken, not to allow anything but liquid to go into the sink drain there will be an amount of greasy matter that will cling to the pipes and clog them unless something more effective than hot water is used for them.

It is an excellent idea to print something like the following on a placard and hang it over the kitchen sink.

Dissolve a tablespoonful of washing soda in two quarts of boiling water, and pour it down the pipe, every day after washing the dinner dishes.

This will be a constant reminder to the one whose province it is to attend to the matter, and it will keep the pipe from getting clogged with grease.

From lack of education many housekeepers do not know that the chemical action of the various liquids that pass through the pipe, make a coating on the inside of it, which is often odorless, but is deadly in its poisonous properties.

It is the duty of every housekeeper to keep her sink under strict surveillance and to insist that it be kept perfectly neat and clean.

It is not sufficient that the outside be examined,

or that the sink is free from slops or grease; the closet underneath, if there be one, is what will require particular attention, and a constant watch kept for mouldering rags, from which poisonous gases will permeate the house and affect the health of all its inmates.

This closet should be thoroughly washed out with strong hot suds once a week and the door left open to dry it, and no kettle, or cooking implement should be kept there, and no refuse pail should be allowed. The plan of keeping a small one here, to be emptied perhaps once a day is often devised by the maid in order to save herself steps, but it should not be permitted.

It will save a housekeeper much annoyance if she can have this sink closet entirely removed. The pipes underneath may not look ornamental, but they can easily be painted and a mistress can rest secure in the thought that at least there is one less point to demand close attention and watchful care.

CHAPTER XV.

THE CARE OF LAMPS.

THE general use of lamps at the present time makes a knowledge of the care of them very important.

A new lamp or burner may be neglected for a time and yet burn very well—but it is not safe to do this with an old one.

There is nothing that adds more to the comfort and cheerfulness of a room at night than a brilliant light, and care should be used in selecting a lamp, to purchase only such as have the best burner that the market affords. Economize if need be in the style and pattern of the lamp rather than the burner.

Have on hand a good supply of wicks and put in fresh ones as soon as the light begins to grow dim, after it has been turned up to the proper height. Be careful that the wicks always fit exactly, that they are not too large, too small, or too thin for the burner.

Use the best oil that can be purchased, and keep it in a tightly closed can. If the oil is exposed to the air it will give a dull light, and the wicks will crust over shortly after they are lighted.

If the oil is exposed to a light from a match, candle, gas or other burner, there is great danger of explosion, and a mistress should impress this firmly upon her maid.

The care of lamps is quite an item in the daily routine, and if there is but one maid for the family service, they are very apt to be neglected for want of intelligent care, unless the mistress takes this duty upon herself.

When there is a waitress employed, the care of the lamps falls to her, and full directions for systematic care of them should be given by the mistress in the beginning.

A large tin tray for holding oil can, cloths,

scissors, case knife, etc., will be found convenient for keeping the materials together, and for holding the lamps as they are filled.

The lamps should be filled with oil every morning, and once a week emptied out, and the oil at the bottom that looks as if there was a sediment of dirt in it should be thrown away.

Wipe them carefully, first with a damp cloth and then with a soft dry one.

Lift off the top of the wick carefully with a dry cloth, being careful not to let any fall on the burner. Do not use the scissors for this purpose, except occasionally, if you would have the best results.

Turn the wick down into the burner a little way, and wipe the edge and sides thoroughly, and leave them so. If they remain above the burner, the wick acts as a sort of siphon, allowing the oil to draw up and run over the edge and down the burner even to the lamp—causing a disagreeable odor, even when the lamp is not lighted.

Use a toothpick or a hairpin for cleaning out

every hole in the burners, for if these become clogged you cannot have a bright light, because these small perforations are necessary for just the right circulation of air.

Wash the chimneys in hot soap suds, wipe and polish them with a dry linen towel. Many use old soft newspapers for this purpose. A piece of sponge fastened to a stick is a good thing to clean lamp chimneys with.

As often as once a month it is well to boil the burners for a few minutes in soda and water, or water in which there is a little ammonia. After boiling; if they are rubbed with a little sapolio and a flannel cloth they will look bright and new, and you will not be annoyed with a disagreeable odor or a poor light.

Metallic lamps should be cleaned by wiping with a damp cloth, and polishing with a piece of chamois skin.

Hand lamps that must be carried about the house should be made of metal. Glass or porcelain lamps should never be used for this purpose.

Often for economy when a lamp must be kept burning through the night, the wick is turned down, leaving only a dim light.

This is a mistake, for the mechanism of the lamp is such that it is intended to burn with the flame at full heat. If the wick is turned low, more gas is generated than with a full blaze, and it becomes a distinct source of danger, as it is the gas, and not the oil, that explodes.

There is no danger from a properly ventilated, clean lamp more than half filled with good oil and burning with its full light. But a sudden jar or fall of a lamp in which the oil is nearly burned out, or in which ventilation is obstructed by charred bits of wick, dirt, or dust, has been the cause of many accidents, and every housekeeper should realize this and feel it an imperative duty to see that each lamp receives proper care and attention.

CHAPTER XVI.

HOUSE CLEANING.

IN all households there are certain periods in which the comfort of the family is subordinate to the good of the house. Custom has appointed the spring as the annual time for renovating and cleansing, but it is as often needed in the fall, for the destruction of the microbes and germs, which have made their way during the hot weather into the house through various agencies.

Certain housekeepers take work as some children do the measles,—"hard." Others can go through with a vast amount, without allowing the machinery to be visible.

There is no need of turning everything upside down at once. Clean little by little, finishing one room before beginning another, even if it is more convenient to have all the carpets taken up at the same time.

And just here let me put in a plea for the rug and the painted or hard wood floor. Think what a saving in time, strength and expense, to take the rugs into the open air, beat them on the grass or clothes line, wash or polish the floor, and that part of the work is over—no buffalo bugs to fight in the corners or along the edges.

Before the weather becomes warm enough for the actual cleaning to commence give your attention to the closets.

Remove the woollen gowns, search thoroughly for moth-eggs, shake and brush well. All flannel undergarments must undergo the same inspection.

Do not be afraid to give away or sell cast-off clothing for which you have no need. Too much trash is carefully hoarded each year, on the chance that "it may come handy some day," and old clothing is stored away in drawers and boxes to become a nest in which moths may breed, which ought to have been given away.

If there are drawers in the closet or if the shelves are movable, take them out, wash, and dry in the sun, and set one side, until the wall, floor and nails of the closet, have been wiped with a cloth wrung out in hot water. Leave the door wide open, that the dampness may be gone before you return your garments to their accustomed places.

If you have ever been troubled with either moths or buffalo bugs, the closets should receive most thorough care and attention. Every drawer and shelf should be removed, thoroughly examined, washed with hot water and soap, and a mixture of one gallon of benzine, and one ounce of carbolic acid, applied. This should also be used for the cleats upon which they rest, and corners and crevices should also be saturated with it.

There should not be any carpet on the closet floors, not even a mat. If there are cracks, they should be scalded thoroughly, and filled with putty. The floor can then be painted or stained.

If there are broken places or cracks in the

walls, fill them with plaster of Paris stirred to a thick paste with cold water.

The walls should be brushed down with a broom over which soft cloth has been pinned, and these may afterwards be wiped off in the same way with a damp cloth. Be careful to leave the closet door open until everything is thoroughly dry, before replacing the contents of shelves and drawers, or hanging anything on the hooks.

Early in February it is well to examine the sunny windows in the house, especially the attic windows for the little red and black buffalo beetle which bears such a strong resemblance to the lady bug.

After the linen closet has been thoroughly cleaned, it is well to ascertain just what has become worn and needs to be replenished in both table and bed linen.

After the closets, the bureau drawers and trunks usually receive attention. The drawers in your bureau, commode or chiffoniére should be removed, and the inside of the different pieces of furniture carefully cleaned. If you discover any traces of moth, blow a liberal supply of Persian insect powder into every crack and crevice. Brush and wipe out each drawer with a damp cloth.

If any article of furniture needs to be repaired or upholstered, it is well to have it attended to, before commencing upon the rooms. When there are carpets to be taken up, and the buffalo bug has appeared in them, benzine should be used freely.

The grubs of the beetle are little hairy creatures, so small that they can easily hide in the fuzz of the carpet. They should be fought persistently before they turn into chrysalis form, and fly away as beetles.

It is the worm-like grub that eats the carpets and does so much mischief, and not the beetle. The beetle however must be fought, in order that it may have no chance to enter the house, and lay a new generation of grubs.

A carpet infested with these grubs should be thoroughly shaken, cleaned, and saturated about the edges, with the preparation of benzine and carbolic acid, previously referred to.

It should be dry before it is relaid, and should not be closely tacked to the floor, only sufficient to keep it in place, as it will need constant attention until all the moths have been destroyed.

Carpets should be taken up, and shaken once a year. They will wear longer by so doing, as the dust which collects under them grinds out the threads.

A carpet should be beaten on both sides; the wrong side first. If badly soiled, it can be cleaned with warm water, to which has been added borax in the proportion of two tablespoonfuls of borax to a pail of water. A scrubbing brush can be used if necessary. It should be rinsed and wiped dry afterwards.

If the carpet shows signs of daily wear, the breadths may be ripped apart and reversed, to bring the wear in a different place.

Matting, as most housekeepers know, should never be soaped. Take it up, sweep and dust it well on both sides, then wipe it with a clean cloth wrung out in salt and water, rubbing it dry as quickly as you can, so that it may retain none of the moisture. The same remark applies to the cleaning of wicker work.

Oil-cloths, linoleum and other floor-cloths can be kept bright by washing with equal quantities of milk and water. Once in several months a little linseed oil or beeswax in spirits of turpentine may be used.

After the carpet is taken up, the stuffed furniture is beaten with a rattan beater, thoroughly brushed, and the smaller articles of furniture placed in another room—the larger ones being covered with furniture cloths. The pictures should be taken down, dusted and wiped with a damp cloth.

The wood finish and walls of the room should be thoroughly dusted, especially the tops of the windows, doors, picture rail, and base boards.

The floor should be washed first, afterwards the painted woodwork in water in which there is a little ammonia, and the floor scrubbed if of plain pine boards.

If the woodwork is stained and finished instead of painted, put a tablespoon of kerosene into some tepid water, wring your cloth dry and go all over the woodwork with this, rubbing in the direction of the grain of the wood.

Hard wood and stained wood floors should be treated in the same way.

Windows should be washed after the woodwork is cleaned. Ammonia or kerosene in water will make them bright.

The room is now ready for the carpet, rugs, furniture and pictures.

There are various preparations that can be bought for polishing furniture, but a very simple and satisfactory polish is a mixture of one-third linseed oil and two-thirds turpentine, put in a bottle and shaken before use.

Dust the furniture well, then rub on the mixture with an old piece of flannel: only do a small area at a time, and polish quickly and briskly with two or three soft rubbers, ending up with an old silk handkerchief.

This home-made preparation both cleans and polishes, and does not in time form a sort of cake over the furniture, as do some patent polishes when frequently used.

If the shades are soiled near the bottom, they can be turned and the top placed at the bottom.

If there are stoves to be taken down, remove the nickel trimmings if possible, scour and wrap each piece separately in paper and lay in a dry place.

Mattresses and pillows should be taken out doors and beaten; pillows should not be placed where the sun will shine on them as it will draw out the oil in the feathers.

Bedsteads should be taken down, and the slats and crevices washed with hot water and soap.

If there is any suspicion of bugs, corrosive sublimate dissolved in alcohol should be applied by means of a small sponge.

It is a deadly poison and care should be taken

in using it and afterwards in keeping it out of the reach of children.

Because it is a poison, many housekeepers are using a solution of alum in hot water, all that it will dissolve—with satisfactory results. It must be applied hot, and can not be used on any varnished surface.

For the summer months if you cannot afford screens at your windows, use black mosquito netting, and tack it on before the flies begin to come in the house. It will look better if tacked inside the window casing than when put on the outside. The netting can be left unfastened at the bottom to allow of opening and closing the blinds.

It is a better way if possible to clean one room at a time; commencing up stairs and going right through to the cellar—the halls to be attended to after the rooms are done. But many housekeepers prefer to have all the carpets removed and shaken at once—this may be a more expeditious way but it is hardly as pleasant for the family to have the entire household in confusion for several days without a nook or a corner that looks homelike and comfortable.

In no part of the house is there greater need of a thorough cleaning than the cellar. This should be done every spring and fall. The walls should be thoroughly swept down and a coat of whitewash applied in the spring.

If a cellar bottom is of earth and has boards laid down for walking on, have them carried out doors and swept, washed and dried in the sun before replacing them.

Sweep the floor carefully, in every corner, and sprinkle it with a solution of copperas. Open all the doors and windows and let the air and sunlight penetrate to the remotest corners.

There are few housekeepers who realize the danger that lurks in a cellar, or how important it is that frequent examination and attention be given it throughout the year. Many lives have been lost by disease that has been traced to the cellar.

There is always more or less typhoid fever every fall in country villages, as well as in cities, and if people would look to their wells, their drain pipes, and cellars, during the year, the cause of the evil might often be found.

The potato bin should be looked over frequently —decaying vegetable matter under the living rooms will work mischief in the household.

I have in mind a farm house, the cellar of which has been a receptacle for potatoes and other vegetables for fifty years.

Every summer the toadstools spring up in a night in the crannies between the stone steps of the bulkhead of the cellar, and every winter, for the last six years, there have been cases of sore throat and diphtheria in that house, and it was not until the physician urged the removal of the vegetable cellar that the people themselves had any suspicion of the danger they were in.

With farm houses where there is plenty of land a vegetable cellar built outside the house is an excellent thing. This may not be possible for most of my readers, but care and attention to the house cellar can be given by housewives whose duty it is to see that decayed vegetable matter is not allowed to remain underneath their living rooms.

Care should be given to the ventilation. Windows should be kept open through the day especially during the warm weather.

Windows that are hung on hinges can be opened their entire extent. If they are too high to be easily reached, an old chair or a box strong enough to bear one's weight, should be kept under each one, and a strong catch for holding the window up will be found necessary. There should be a netting outside, that no animal can enter or leaves blow in.

Just before the spring cleaning is the time to have furnace pipes cleaned out, the chimneys attended to and the range put in order. This work is very often deferred till the autumn, and the dust and débris which will sometimes collect in the best-kept heater and registers sift through the house all summer, leaving a thin layer of dust over everything that is exceedingly disagreeable.

It is always best to have a man come to do this

work, but it is also necessary to keep some watch over him to see that he does it properly. All the registers of the house should be taken out, and the pipes conveying the heat brushed out with long-handled brooms.

In all well-regulated families the dusting out of the register is a part of the weekly sweeping, and registers on the floor should be lifted out every sweeping day and dusted and washed. This prevents dust and rubbish collecting in such a place, as it will if these precautions are neglected.

Where the registers have been regularly cared for, there will be no great upheaval of dust at the yearly cleaning, when the pipes are brushed out. All parts of the furnace-box and smoke-pipes of the heater must also be swept free from soot when it is cleaned.

To find out whether this has been properly done, strike the smoke-pipe, after it is replaced with an iron poker, and if it gives a dull, thudding sound, there is still soot in the pipe; if the pipe is clean it will have a clear, ringing sound.

In the spring many housekeepers have the

pipes of the furnace taken down, cleaned and stored in the attic until fall, as the soot is apt to gather moisture, which will cause the pipe to rust.

If there are no open fireplaces or other conveniences for heating the house, during cold, damp weather of the summer, the furnace ought to be left in condition to have a fire made in it at any time.

In the fall before cold weather has set in, the pipes can be taken down and carefully brushed out.

All the registers should be closed and covered over with newspapers or cloths, to prevent the dust from getting into the rooms. The smoke pipe and the flues should be carefully examined, and the former replaced with a new one if the rust has been sufficient to eat the pipe.

Before the winter supply of coal is placed in the cellar see that the fine dust is removed from the bins. If the coal is wet just before it is put in the cellar, it will prevent the dust rising from it and filling the house.

There are many homes throughout the country where well water is used for drinking water as well as for other purposes. Where this is the case, the well itself should be thoroughly cleaned out once a year. During the summer more or less vegetable and animal matter, finding its way into these wells, decays and dies, and after a certain amount of this accumulation, the limited supply of running water, which these receptacles contain, is not sufficient to purify itself, and poisonous germs are taken into the system, which if not sufficiently strong to throw them off, must succumb to disease.

CHAPTER XVII.

THE CARE OF WOOLENS AND FURS.

THE buffalo bug like the common moth prefers wool to any other material, but will not hesitate for any such preference to attack whatever comes in his way whether it be cotton, leather or wool.

They both prefer dust laden and soiled garments to clean ones, consequently every garment that is to be put away for summer, should be placed on the clothes line out-doors, the pockets turned inside out, and should be thoroughly beaten and brushed.

If the material is such as will bear sponging, take a quart of warm water to which has been added about a tablespoonful of turpentine, and go over each article carefully.

After they are dried, sprinkle with camphor or

whole cloves and do them up in newspapers and place them in trunks or drawers which are lined with newspapers, with a covering of the same over the top.

Portieres and heavy drapery curtains should be hung on the line, carefully brushed and placed between layers of newspapers, the edges of which can be carefully pasted together.

Blankets should be washed and cared for in the same way.

Furs ought to be put away for summer before the moth miller makes its appearance.

Select a clear day, with fresh strong wind blowing from the west if possible, and hang your furs on a clothes line out-doors, preparatory to packing them away for the summer.

The dust and dirt should be thoroughly beaten from them, and if you have one of the rattan frames, called "spankers," it will be of great assistance; failing this, smooth, pliable saplings will answer. Have plenty of old newspapers on hand, as experienced housekeepers say that printer's ink is a protection against the moth.

The ordinary manner of packing furs is to fold flat, and place in boxes. This is a mistake, especially with seal garments, as the pressure, although slight, when continued through several months, tends to give a crushed look to the garment.

Furriers keep their garments hanging, and ladies should do likewise. Place them on coat-hangers, which support the shoulders, and prevent the garment from dragging its weight upon the neck and collar, thus injuring the shape. A home-made support of bent wire, or a thin piece of wood whittled to shape, will answer.

Over the garment slip a case made with three thicknesses of newspaper pasted together. Sprinkle borax or Dalmatian powder thickly over the bottom; baste at the top, leaving only space for the string attached to the support, and over this slip another case made of unbleached cotton stitched tightly. Sew this firmly across the top, leaving the string outside to hang it up.

Mothaline bags can be purchased ready-made for this purpose from 60 cents to $1.00, or the cloth for making them at 25 cents per yard. Tarred paper bags are also serviceable.

A muff can be protected in the same way by attaching a long loop from one end to suspend it by. Boas should have strings tacked at the ends and in the middle, in order that the strain may not rest wholly on any one point. Shake them upside down, which will cause the fur to stand out in a round, fluffy manner.

Furs which have been wet ought never to be dried in a warm room. Furriers urge that furs needing repairs should be brought to them in the summer season, as the work can then be done with more convenience to themselves, and at less expense to the wearer.

After the woolen clothing and furs have been packed away through the spring, they will need to be thoroughly aired before they can be used again in the fall. They should be placed on the clothes line, and then shaken and beaten. Let them air through several hours of a bright windy day, and they can then be placed in the closets and drawers where they belong.

CHAPTER XVIII.

SUNDAY DINNER AND TEA.

THE problem of arranging the "Sunday dinner" is one which perplexes many housekeepers.

In a large number of families it is the only day in the week that the husband and father takes his midday meal with them, and naturally it is desired to have it especially enjoyable.

But, on the other hand, it is a day that the maid must be regarded, also. As far as possible it should be a day of rest to her, and a conscientious mistress will so order her household duties that her maid can attend church sometime during the day, even if she is unable to give her the entire afternoon and evening which is so often claimed.

A mother with young children needs all the tact and management that she is capable of, to get through the day so that it may be one to be enjoyed and looked forward to as the happiest one in the week, which in theory we know it should be, but which in practice is often the reverse.

If we would commence to prepare for our Sundays on Saturday, it might simplify the question and be of great assistance.

This Saturday preparation does not mean a cold Sunday dinner, or a warmed-over dinner; in place of that it should be made especially good, for by judicious forethought on Saturday one can select dishes that could be quickly cooked, a dessert that could be made the day before, and an additional delicacy might be added for this dessert which requires no cooking, such as nuts and raisins, or confectionery, or fruit.

Pretty little fancy dishes, that are not used through the week, will help make the table attractive, and one or two flowers with a cluster of green leaves will give a touch of refinement and brighten even the plainest-looking table.

Changes in the table linen through the week should be made with a view to having it perfectly fresh and clean for Sunday.

In our own family our Sunday tea was prepared Sunday morning, before breakfast. Thin bread and butter sandwiches were made, from which the crusts were removed and kept for bread puddings; the sandwiches were cut sometime, into fanciful shapes such as triangles, or into long and narrow strips, and piled up in log-cabin style on a bread-plate, covered with a pretty doily.

Maccaroons, cocoanut cakes and squares of cake were piled in the cake-basket, and these were then placed in a stone crock until tea-time to keep from drying, and a bowl of whipped cream for our chocolate was put into the ice-chest.

This simple little "picnic" tea, as we called it, was served in our drawing-room entirely by the children, an easy-chair for mother being pushed close to a small round table, from which she poured the chocolate and the younger children passed it around to us. It was the most enjoyable meal of the whole week, and we always looked forward to it.

Cold, snowy Sundays it was the perfection of inward harmony and comfort, with a big log crackling in the grate, and mother declared that she never knew anything to equal our appetites for bread and butter sandwiches.

The children cleared everything away; washed the cups and plates, and brushed up whatever crumbs there were on the floor, as the maids were allowed to go out every Sunday afternoon, and mother was never called upon to do anything but pour the chocolate.

There are many things besides the meals that might be planned for as a help to the day.

If the customary change of clothing for each member of the family is taken from bureau or closet and laid carefully on a chair in the bedrooms, before going to bed Saturday night, with buttons all on, rents repaired, spots removed from dress and cloaks, shoes blackened, and fresh ruffs basted in neck and sleeves, much will have been done to ensure happiness and peace of mind for the coming day, and we shall have more time to think how we can make the day brighter for the others by striving to make our tones and manners more gentle and affectionate, and to give expression to the love and good-will in our hearts for the dear ones in our home.

CHAPTER XIX.

THINGS WORTH KNOWING.

DANGER IN PLATED WARE.

THE silver-plated ware that is seen on most tables, is as dangerous after the plate has become partly worn as are the tin fruit cans.

During the sultry dog-day weather of August, if you will unscrew the plated top of any of the fancy salt-holders that have been filled with salt for a few days, there will be found on the inside of this cover a collection of green salt, covered with verdigris from the metal, which is a dangerous poison.

Unless one can afford to have solid silver tops for these holders, it would be better to dispense with them altogether and use the open salt cellar or individual salts.

Do not trust plated silver ware ; after the plate is worn, if you cannot replace it with solid silver, at least have it replated as soon as possible.

TO CLEAN SILVER.

The *Jeweler's Circular* gives the following directions for cleaning silver :—

"Take either a small sponge, a piece of flannel, a piece of chamois, or a clean and dry silver brush ; rub all the articles which have bad spots with salt. This removes the spots more quickly than anything else. The simplest method is to place a little prepared chalk in a saucer with water, of which make a thick paste, and add a few drops of ammonia. In place of ammonia, the chalk can be prepared with alcohol or simply with water. This paste is to be brushed or rubbed carefully over the article."

HOW TO WASH WINDOWS.

Do not wash windows when the sun is shining on them, as they will look cloudy and streaky from drying before they are well polished.

The glass and sash should be first dusted, and the window first washed on the inside with water which has a little ammonia in it. Rinse them and wipe with an old soft cloth which is free from lint, as soon as possible after washing, and polish with newspaper or chamois skin. For the corners a small brush, or pointed stick with an end of the cloth may be used.

HOW TO TEST THE HEAT OF AN OVEN.

To judge of an oven's heat there are no better rules than Gouffe's: "Try the oven every ten minutes with a piece of white paper. If too hot the paper will blaze up or blacken; when the paper becomes dark brown (rather darker than ordinary meat pie crust) the oven is fit for small pastry. When light brown (the color of really nice pastry), it is ready for vol au vent tarts, etc. When the paper turns dark yellow, you can bake bread, large meat pies or large pound cakes; while if it is just tinged, the oven is just fit for sponge cake, meringues, etc.

HOW TO FUMIGATE A ROOM.

After an illness in the house it is always wise to fumigate, and if the disease is of a contagious nature it is a necessity. The following rules for fumigating a room are given by the *Journal of Health.*

The doors, windows, fireplace, etc., should be closed. Paste strips of paper over all the cracks. Fumigation by burning sulphur is most easily accomplished.

Two pounds of sulphur should be allowed for every room from ten to twelve feet square.

It is better to divide it up and put it in several pans, rather than burn the entire quantity of sulphur used in one pan. To avoid the danger of fire, these pans should be set on bricks, or in other and larger pans filled with water or with sand.

After pouring a little alcohol on the sulphur, and properly placing the pans about the room, the farthest from the door of exit should be lighted first; the others in order.

The operator will need to move quickly, for no one can breathe sulphurous fumes with safety.

After closing the door, the cracks around it should be pasted up, as was done within the room.

Six hours, at least, is generally necessary to fumigate a room properly; at the end of that time it may be entered and the windows opened, and they should be left open as long as is convenient, even for a week, if possible.

After fumigation, a thorough process of cleansing should be instituted. At least, the walls and ceiling should be rubbed dry; much the better way is to whitewash and repaper.

The floor and the woodwork and the furniture should be scrubbed with a solution of carbolic acid, or some other disinfectant.

"A pinch of sulphur thrown upon the kitchen range every day would do much to keep a family in good health."

THE MATTRESS.

The spiral springs on beds injure the mattress unless it is covered. If they do not rust it, the pressure on the iron rings soon wears it, no matter how frequently it may be turned. The mattress should be covered with stout unbleached cotton, if it is not made in separate pieces. or a comfortable should be placed between the springs and the mattress.

If a cover is used, make it so that one side shall be left open to admit the mattress, and fasten it together with buttons and buttonholes. In this way the cover may be easily removed and washed when so desired. These covers are nice for single mattresses made in one piece.

This covering may be made of a light grade of ticking in place of the unbleached cotton.

The ticking is stouter, and protects the mattress better from the wear of the springs.

If you wish to clean an old mattress, take some clear warm water, add a few drops of ammonia, enough to make the water feel smooth; then, with a clean cloth and white castlle soap, wash the spots, rinse in clear water, and rub well with a dry cloth.

Use only enough water to dampen the spots. If that does not remove them, dip the cloth in pure ammonia, rub hard, then rinse in clear water and dry.

A mattress should be turned frequently from side to side and from head to foot, to insure its wearing evenly. Most people are familiar with mattresses sagged at one end, but may not know that this is due to neglect in turning. They should be well aired each day, and the dust removed from the top by brushing well with a whisk-broom.

Most mattresses for double beds are now made in two parts, and some even in three sections. This permits a more even wear, and they are also much more easily turned and cared for.

THE ICE CHEST.

Wash every part of the ice chest thoroughly, twice a week with hot water and washing soda, pouring some of the boiling hot soda down the pipe. Run a long wire with a sponge tied to the end, down the pipe before washing it, in order to clear the slimy substance that often gathers there and clogs it. See that no scraps are allowed to stand in the ice chest. Do not keep the milk and butter with meat or with anything that can taint it; remember that milk and butter absorb odors very quickly. If there is a pan to be emptied under the ice chest, it should be attended to regularly night and morning, and washed and wiped out each time.

CHAPTER XX.

BITS OF EXPERIENCE.

TO loosen the cover of a fruit jar that has become stuck, invert the jar and place the top in hot water for a few moments.

Vaseline will soften boots and shoes that have been hardened by water, and render them as pliable as new.

If a bedstead creaks at each movement of the sleeper, remove the slats and wrap the ends of each in old newspapers.

Stains and grease may be removed from a carpet. A mixture which is excellent for removing grease spots and stains from the carpet and clothing is made from two ounces of ammonia, two ounces of white castile soap, one ounce of glycerine, one ounce of ether; cut the soap fine;

dissolve in one pint of water over the fire; add two quarts of rain water. Other spots in silk are to be rubbed gently with a linen rag dipped in this mixture.

If the globes on a gas fixture are much stained on the outside by smoke, soak them in tolerably hot water, in which a little washing-soda has been dissolved. Then put a teaspoon of powdered ammonia in a pan of lukewarm water, and with a hard brush scrub the globes until the smoke stains disappear. Rinse in clean, cold water. They will be as white as if new.

Long bags, the full length of dress or cloak, with hanging loops at the top, save from creasing as well as from dust and moths.

The best thing to clean tinware is common soda; rub on briskly with a damp cloth, after which, wipe dry.

To clean ornaments of alabaster dissolve borax in boiling water and apply with a cloth or soft brush; rinse carefully and dry in the sun.

Give oil-cloth a light coat of varnish when it

is put down, and renew the varnish before the oil-cloth gets dingy. This care will keep it bright, and it will also last much longer.

By rubbing with a flannel dipped in whiting, the brown discoloration may be taken off cups which have been used for baking.

A good furniture varnish is made of two ounces white wax, one gill of oil of turpentine; melt the wax, and gradually mix in the turpentine.

Clean your plaster casts by making some cold starch and dipping them into it, brushing when dry.

Paper bags, in which many articles are sent from grocers, should be saved for use when blacking a stove. The hand can be slipped into one of these and the brush handled just as well, and the hands will not be soiled.

Common salt is said to be one of the best agents for cleaning marble, such as wash-basins, sink-fixtures, and the like. It requires no preparation, and may be rubbed directly upon the tarnished surface, removing any incrustations or deposits at once, leaving the marble shining and clean.

To clean decanters, take soft brown or blotting-paper, wet and soap it, and roll it up into small pieces, and put the pieces into the decanter with a little warm water, shake well, and rinse with clear, cold water; wipe the outside with a dry, soft cloth, and let the decanter drain.

Many are the bits of soap which are wasted in the household. A good plan is to save every scrap in a jar or keg, and when wanted cover them with water, and set them on the stove to simmer. When melted, remove them and let them get cold. Crumbs made in cutting up soap, bits of toilet soap too small to use, all such odds and ends can be saved and used in this manner.

Borax water will remove all soils and stains from the hands, and is said to heal all scratches and chafes. To make it, put crude borax into a bottle and fill it with hot water. When the borax is dissolved add more to the water, until at last the water can absorb no more, and a residuum remains at the bottom of the bottle. To the water in which the hands are to be washed, pour from this bottle to make it very soft. It is very cleansing, and by its use the hands will be kept in excellent condition.

To clean a gilt picture frame, wash the surface with a sponge, lightly saturated with hot spirits of wine or oil of turpentine. There must be no wiping, but the moisture must be left to dry.

If your coal fire is low, a tablespoon of salt thrown on it will help it very much.

Instead of putting food into the oven to keep hot for late comers, try covering it closely with a tin, and setting it over a basin of hot water. This plan will keep the food hot, and at the same time prevent it from drying.

A few drops of ammonia in the bath will render the water soft as rain-water.

For cleaning paint it should be used in about the proportion of a tablespoon to a quart of warm water.

There is nothing better than a weak solution of ammonia and water for washing looking-glasses, window-glass, lamp chimneys, etc.

To remove ink from cotton, silk or woollen goods, saturate the spot with spirits of turpentine and let it remain several hours, then rub between the hands. It will crumble away without injuring the color or texture of the article.

Finely sifted wood ashes will remove medicine stains from silver spoons. Egg stains on silver can be taken off with fine salt and damp cloth.

A good mixture to have in the house is composed of aqua ammonia, two ounces; soft water, one quart; saltpetre, one teaspoonful; shaving soap one ounce. Scrape the soap fine before mixing the other ingredients, and allow it to stand a few hours before using. It will remove grease and other stains from woollen fabrics and is excellent for sponging coats and vests that have become worn and shiny looking. Rub it in thoroughly with a cloth wet with the mixture, and then wash it off with clear cold water.

To remove paper labels from old bottles, wet the face of the label with water and hold it for an instant over any convenient flame. The steam penetrates the label at once and softens the paste.

To keep the bread-jar and cake-box sweet, rinse after washing with boiling water in which a little common soda has been dissolved; then set out-of-doors in the sun for a few hours.

Chloride of lime will often prove a preventive for rats, and they will flee from its odor as from a pestilence. It should be thrown down their holes and spread about wherever they are likely to come, and should be renewed once in a fortnight.

Powdered borax is a prevention for water bugs and cockroaches. Sprinkle about the sink and water pipes,—in a few days they will disappear.

CHAPTER XXI.

IN THE WAY OF ADVICE.

THE faculty of making a little go a great way, of economizing not only with money, but with time, that the twenty-four hours may be sufficient for other duties besides those of housekeeping—is of real worth to any woman.

Those who possess this faculty by nature, are fitted to become successful housekeepers, in whatever condition of life they may be placed.

Those who do not possess it should make every effort to acquire it, for the sake of their family, and for their own individual comfort and happiness.

System and planning—the significance of these two words is equally as important to the housewife as to the man or woman in business life.

To be able to make investment of the money set aside for household expenses, in a way that the family may receive the most value from it, is something to be proud of.

To furnish one's home with plain substantial furniture that can be easily kept clean, to eliminate the element of pretension from it, and yet to express refinement, comfort and individuality, is something to be proud of.

There are many ways that may be planned to save steps and labor. The over-worked, nervous housewife especially, should bend all her energies to this end. For such a one it is not necessary to follow out to the letter, the details as given in this or any other work on the subject, if by so doing she must tax her health, or narrow her life to the mere routine of household drudgery.

But sufficient thought must be given that she may know where and when to slight her work, and still secure comfort for her household.

When a woman plans to do too much in one day, and gets dissatisfied with herself and all her family because she does not get through with it all in that time, nerves are usually at the bottom of it all.

When a naturally good-natured little mother begins to grow irritable, and cannot bear the noise of the children's laughter, and jumps with fright if the door bangs, it is likely to be a case of "The Nerves," and when she tells the little ones that she is too tired to answer questions, and can't have them playing in the room with her and hurries them out of it before they have time to argue it a bit, it is a clear case, for even the children understand it, and agree among themselves that mamma is "cross" to-day and has got "the nervous" pretty bad, and carry off their treasures and their troubles to more remote quarters.

Now if that little mother, with all her sister housekeepers who are troubled with this disease, will seat herself occasionally through the day in the most comfortable chair she possesses, throw her head against the back of it, relax every tired and strained muscle in her body until head, arms and legs hang off from her like dead-weights, and sit there for fifteen minutes, it will do her more good than all the tonics that by and by the doctors are going to prescribe for her. Let her follow up this idea, varying it occasionally with a glance through the latest magazine or book at the time when she feels most tired and hurried, and she may save herself considerable suffering and unhappiness later on, as well as general discomfort and anxiety for her family.

www.ingramcontent.com/pod-product-compliance
Lightning Source LLC
LaVergne TN
LVHW011234110826
845150LV00006B/1634
9781425572266